Modernizing Legacy Applications in PHP

Get your code under control in a
series of small, specific steps

Paul M. Jones

Packt>

BIRMINGHAM - MUMBAI

Modernizing Legacy Applications in PHP

First published: August 2016

Production reference: 1260816

Published by Packt Publishing Ltd.
Livery Place
35 Livery Street
Birmingham B3 2PB, UK.

ISBN 978-1-78712-470-7

www.packtpub.com

Credits

Author
Paul M. Jones

Acquisition Editor
Frank Pohlmann

Technical Editor
Danish Shaikh

Indexer
Mariammal Chettiyar

Graphics
Disha Haria

Production Coordinator
Arvindkumar Gupta

Cover Work
Arvindkumar Gupta

Foreword

In early 2012, while attending a popular PHP conference in Chicago, I approached a good friend, Paul Jones, with questions about PSR-0 and autoloading. We immediately broke out my laptop to view an attempt at applying the convention and Paul really helped me put the pieces together in short order. His willingness to jump right in and help others always inspires me, and has gained my respect.

So in August of 2012 I heard of a video containing a talk given by Paul at the Nashville PHP User Group, and was drawn in. The talk, *It Was Like That When I Got Here: Steps Toward Modernizing A Legacy Codebase*, sounded interesting because it highlighted something I am passionate about: refactoring.

After watching I was electrified! I often speak about refactoring and receive inquiries on how to apply it for legacy code rather than performing a rewrite. Put another way, how is refactoring possible in a codebase where includes and requires are the norm, namespaces don't exist, globals are used heavily, and object instantiation runs rampant with no dependency injection? And what if the codebase is procedural?

Paul's focus of modernizing a legacy application filled the gap by getting legacy code to a point where standard refactoring is possible. His step-by-step approach makes it easier for developers to *get the bear dancing* so continued improving of code through refactoring can happen.

I felt the topic was a must see for PHP developers and quickly fired off an email asking if he'd be interested in flying to Miami and giving the same talk for the South Florida PHP User Group. Within minutes my email was answered and Paul even offered to drive down from Nashville for the talk. However, since I started organizing the annual *SunshinePHP Developer Conference* to be held February in Miami we decided to have Paul speak at the conference rather than come down earlier.

Fast forward two years later, and here we are in mid-2014. Developing with PHP has really matured in recent years, but it's no secret that PHP's low level of entry for beginners helped create some nasty codebases. Companies who built applications in the dark times simply can't afford to put things on hold and rebuild a legacy application, especially with today's fast paced economy and higher developer salaries. To stay competitive, companies must continually push developers for new features and to increase application stability. This creates a hostile environment for developers working with a poorly written legacy application. Modernizing a legacy application is a necessity, and must happen. Yet knowing how to create clean code and comprehending how to modernize a legacy application are two entirely different things.

Paul and I have been speaking to packed rooms at conferences around the world about modernizing and refactoring. Developers are hungry for knowledge on how to improve the quality of their code and perfect their craft. Unfortunately, we can only reach a small portion of PHP developers using these methods. The time has come for us to create books in hopes of reaching more PHP developers to improve the situation.

I see more and more developers embrace refactoring into their development workflow to leverage methods outlined in my talks and forthcoming book *Refactoring 101*. But understanding how to use these refactoring processes on a legacy codebase is not straight forward, and sometimes impossible. The book you're about to read bridges the gap, allowing developers to modernize a codebase so refactoring can be applied for continued enhancement. Many thanks to Paul for putting this together. Enjoy!

Adam Culp

(https://leanpub.com/refactoring101)

About the Author

Paul M. Jones is an internationally recognized PHP expert who has worked as everything from junior developer to VP of Engineering in all kinds of organizations (corporate, military, non-profit, educational, medical, and others). He blogs professionally at `www.paul-m-jones.com` and is a regular speaker at various PHP conferences.

Paul's latest open-source project is Aura for PHP. Previously, he was the architect behind the Solar Framework, and was the creator of the Savant template system. He was a founding contributor to the Zend Framework (the DB, DB_Table, and View components), and has written a series of authoritative benchmarks on dynamic framework performance.

Paul was one of the first elected members of the PEAR project. He is a voting member of the PHP Framework Interoperability Group, where he shepherded the PSR-1 *Coding Standard* and PSR-2 *Coding Style* recommendations, and was the primary author on the PSR-4 *Autoloader* recommendation. He was also a member of the Zend PHP 5.3 Certification education advisory board.

In a previous career, Paul was an operations intelligence specialist for the US Air Force. In his spare time, he enjoys putting .308 holes in targets at 400 yards.

Acknowledgement

Many thanks to all of the conference attendees who heard my *It Was Like That When I Got Here* presentation and who encouraged me to expand it into a full book. Without you, I would not have considered writing this at all.

Thank you to Adam Culp, who provided a thorough review of the work-in-progress, and for his concentration on refactoring approaches. Thanks also to Chris Hartjes, who went over the chapter on unit testing in depth and gave it his blessing. Many thanks to Luis Cordova, who acted as a work-in-progress editor and who corrected my many pronoun issues.

Finally, thanks to everyone who bought a copy of the book before it was complete, and especially to those who provided feedback and insightful questions regarding it. These include Hari KT (a long-time colleague on the Aura project), Ron Emaus, Gareth Evans, Jason Fuller, David Hurley, Stephen Lawrence, Elizabeth Tucker

Long, Chris Smith, and others too numerous to name. Your early support helped to assure me that writing the book was worthwhile.

www.PacktPub.com

eBooks, discount offers, and more

Did you know that Packt offers eBook versions of every book published, with PDF and ePub files available? You can upgrade to the eBook version at www.PacktPub.com and as a print book customer, you are entitled to a discount on the eBook copy. Get in touch with us at customercare@packtpub.com for more details.

At www.PacktPub.com, you can also read a collection of free technical articles, sign up for a range of free newsletters and receive exclusive discounts and offers on Packt books and eBooks.

PACKT ™

https://www2.packtpub.com/books/subscription/packtlib

Do you need instant solutions to your IT questions? PacktLib is Packt's online digital book library. Here, you can search, access, and read Packt's entire library of books.

Why subscribe?

- Fully searchable across every book published by Packt
- Copy and paste, print, and bookmark content
- On demand and accessible via a web browser

Table of Contents

Preface

I have been programming professionally in one capacity or another for over 30 years. I continue to find it a challenging and rewarding career. I still learn new lessons about my profession every day, as I think is the case for every programmer dedicated to this craft.

Even more challenging and rewarding is helping other programmers to learn what I have learned. I have worked with PHP for 15 years now, in many different kinds of organizations and in every capacity from junior developer to VP of Engineering. In that time, I have learned a lot about the commonalities in legacy PHP applications. This book is distilled from my notes and memories from modernizing those codebases. I hope it can serve as a path for other programmers to follow, leading them out of a morass of bad code and bad work situations, and into a better life for themselves.

This book also serves as penance for all of the legacy code I have left behind for others to deal with. All I can say is that I didn't know then what I know now. In part, I offer this book as atonement for the coding sins of my past. I hope it can help you to avoid my previous mistakes.

1
Legacy Applications

In its simplest definition, a legacy application is any application that you, as a developer, inherit from someone else. It was written before you arrived, and you had little or no decision-making authority in how it was built.

However, there is a lot more weight to the word legacy among developers. It carries with it connotations of poorly organized, difficult to maintain and improve, hard to understand, untested or untestable, and a series of similar negatives. The application works as a product in that it provides revenue, but as a program, it is brittle and sensitive to change.

Because this is a book specifically about PHP-based legacy applications, I am going to offer some PHP-specific characteristics that I have seen in the field. For our purposes, a legacy application in PHP is one that matches two or more of the following descriptions:

- It uses page scripts placed directly in the document root of the web server.
- It has special index files in some directories to prevent access to those directories.
- It has special logic at the top of some files to `die()` or `exit()` if a certain value is not set.
- Its architecture is include-oriented instead of class-oriented or object-oriented.
- It has relatively few classes.
- Any class structure that exists is disorganized, disjointed, and otherwise inconsistent.
- It relies more heavily on functions than on class methods.
- Its page scripts, classes, and functions combine the concerns of model, view, and controller into the same scope.

- It shows evidence of one or more incomplete attempts at a rewrite, sometimes as a failed framework integration.
- It has no automated test suite for the developers to run.

These characteristics are probably familiar to anyone who has had to deal with a very old PHP application. They describe what I call a typical PHP application.

The typical PHP application

Most PHP developers are not formally trained as programmers, or are almost entirely self-taught. They often come to the language from other, usually non-technical, professions. Somehow or another, they are tasked with the duty of creating webpages because they are seen as the most technically-savvy person in their organization. Since PHP is such a forgiving language and grants a lot of power without a lot of discipline, it is very easy to produce working web pages and even applications without a lot of training.

These and other factors strongly influence the underlying foundation of the typical PHP application. They are usually not written in a popular full-stack framework or even a micro-framework. Instead, they are often a series of page scripts, placed directly in the web server document root, to which clients can browse directly. Any functionality that needs to be reused has been collected into a series of `include` files. There are `include` files for common configurations and settings, headers and footers, common forms and content, function definitions, navigation, and so on.

This reliance on `include` files in the typical PHP application is what makes me call them include-oriented architectures. The legacy application uses `include` calls everywhere to couple the pieces of the program into a single whole. This is in contrast to a class-oriented architecture, where even if the application does not adhere to good object-oriented programming principles, at least the behaviors are bundled into classes.

File Structure

The typical include-oriented PHP application generally looks something like this:

```
/path/to/docroot/
bin/                        # command-line tools
cache/                     # cache files
common/                  # commonly-used include files
classes/                   # custom classes
```

```
Image.php              #
Template.php         #
functions/             # custom functions
db.php                 #
log.php                #
cache.php            #
setup.php              # configuration and setup
css/                     # stylesheets
img/                   # images
index.php            # home page script
js/                      # JavaScript
lib/                     # third-party libraries
log/                   # log files
page1.php          # other page scripts
page2.php        #
page3.php        #
sql/                    # schema migrations
sub/                  # sub-page scripts
index.php        #
subpage1.php #
subpage2.php #
theme/                # site theme files
header.php      # a header template
footer.php       # a footer template
nav.php            # a navigation template ~~
```

The structure shown is a simplified example. There are many possible variations. In some legacy applications, I have seen literally hundreds of main-level page scripts and dozens of subdirectories with their own unique hierarchies for additional pages. The key is that the legacy application is usually in the document root, has page scripts that users browse to directly, and uses include files to manage most program behavior instead of classes and objects.

Page Scripts

Legacy applications will use individual page scripts as the access point for public behavior. Each page script is responsible for setting up the global environment, performing the requested logic, and then delivering output to the client.

Appendix A, Typical Legacy Page Script contains a sanitized, anonymized version of a typical legacy page script from a real application. I have taken the liberty of making the indentation consistent (originally, the indents were somewhat random) and wrapping it at 60 characters so it fits better on e-reader screens. Go take a look at it now, but be careful. I won't be held liable if you go blind or experience post-traumatic stress as a result! As we examine it, we find all manner of issues that make maintenance and improvement difficult:

- The `include` statements to execute setup and presentation logic
- inline function definitions
- global variables
- model, view, and controller logic all combined in a single script
- trusting user input
- possible SQL injection vulnerabilities
- possible cross-site scripting vulnerabilities
- unquoted array keys generating notices
- The `if` blocks not wrapped in braces (adding a line in the block later will not actually be part of the block)
- copy-and-paste repetition

The *Appendix A, Typical Legacy Page Script* example is relatively tame as far as legacy page scripts go. I have seen other scripts where JavaScript and CSS code have been mixed in, along with remote-file inclusions and all sorts of security flaws. It is also only (!) about 400 lines long. I have seen page scripts that are thousands of lines long which generate several different page variations, all wrapped into a single `switch` statement with a dozen or more `case` conditions.

Rewrite or Refactor?

Many developers, when presented with a typical PHP application, are able to live with it for only so long before they want to scrap it and rewrite it from scratch. Nuke it from orbit; it's the only way to be sure! is the rallying cry of these enthusiastic and energetic programmers. Other developers, their enthusiasm drained by their death march experience, feel cautious and wary at such a suggestion. They are fully aware that the codebase is bad, but the devil (or in our case, code) they know is better than the devil they don't.

The Pros and Cons of Rewriting

A complete rewrite is a very tempting idea. Developers championing a rewrite feel like they will be able to do all the right things the first time through. They will be able to write unit tests, enforce best practices, separate concerns according to modern pattern definitions, and use the latest framework or even write their own framework (since they know best what their own needs are). Because the existing application can serve as a reference implementation, they feel confident that there will be little or no trial-and-error work in rewriting the application. The needed behaviors already exist; all the developers need to do is copy them to the new system. The behaviors that are difficult or impossible to implement in the existing system can be added on from the start as part of the rewrite.

As tempting as a rewrite sounds, it is fraught with many dangers. Joel Spolsky had this to say regarding the old Netscape Navigator web browser rewrite in 2000:

> *Netscape made the single worst strategic mistake that any software company can make by deciding to rewrite their code from scratch. Lou Montulli, one of the 5 programming superstars who did the original version of Navigator, emailed me to say, I agree completely, it's one of the major reasons I resigned from Netscape. This one decision cost Netscape 3 years. That's three years in which the company couldn't add new features, couldn't respond to the competitive threads from Internet Explorer, and had to sit on their hands while Microsoft completely ate their lunch.*
>
> *- Joel Spolsky, Netscape Goes Bonkers*

Netscape went out of business as a result.

Josh Kerr relates a similar story regarding TextMate:

> *Macromates, an indie company who had a very successful text editor called Textmate, decided to rewrite the code base for Textmate 2. It took them 6 years to get a beta release out the door which is an eternity in today's time and they lost a lot of market share. When they did release a beta, it was too late and 6 months later they folded the project and pushed it on to Github as an open source project.*
>
> *- Josh Kerr, TextMate 2 And Why You Shouldn't Rewrite Your Code*

Fred Brooks calls the urge to do a complete rewrite the second-system effect. He wrote about this in 1975:

> *The second is the most dangerous system a man ever designs. ... The general tendency is to over-design the second system, using all the ideas and frills that were cautiously sidetracked on the first one. ... The second-system effect has ... a tendency to refine techniques whose very existence has been made obsolete by changes in basic system assumptions. ... How does the project manager avoid the second-system effect? By insisting on a senior architect who has at least two systems under his belt.*

> *- Fred Brooks, The Mythical Man-Month, pp. 53-58.*

Developers were the same forty years ago as they are today. I expect them to be the same over the next forty years as well; human beings remain human beings. Overconfidence, insufficient pessimism, ignorance of history, and the desire to be one's own customer all lead developers easily into rationalizations that this time will be different when they attempt a rewrite.

Why Don't Rewrites Work?

There are lots of reasons why a rewrite rarely works, but I will concentrate on only one general reason here: the intersection of resources, knowledge, communication, and productivity. (Be sure to read *The Mythical Man-Month* (pp. 13-26) for a great description of the problems associated with thinking of resources and scheduling as interchangeable elements.)

As with all things, we have only limited resources to bring to bear against the rewrite project. There are only a certain number of developers in the organization. These are the developers who will have to do *both* maintenance on the existing program *and* write the completely new version of the program. Any developers working on the one project will not be able to work on the other.

The Context-switching problem

One idea is to have the existing developers spend part of their time on the old application and part of their time on the new one. However, moving a developer between the two projects will not be an even split of productivity. Because of the cognitive load of context-switching, the developer will be less than half as productive on each.

The Knowledge problem

To avoid the productivity losses from switching developers between maintenance and the rewrite, the organization may try to hire more developers. Some can then be dedicated to the old project and others to the new project. Unfortunately, this approach reveals what F. A. Hayek calls the knowledge problem. Originally applied to the realm of economics, the knowledge problem applies equally as well to programming.

If we put the new developers on the rewrite project, they won't know enough about the existing system, the existing problems, the business goals, and perhaps not even the best practices for doing the rewrite to be effective. They will have to be trained on these things, most likely by the existing developers. This means the existing developers, who have been relegated to maintaining the existing program, will have to spend a lot of time communicating knowledge to the new hires. The amount of time involved is non-trivial, and the communication of this knowledge will have to continue until the new developers are as well-versed as the existing developers. This means that the linear increase in resources results in a less-than-linear increase in productivity: a 100% increase in the number of programmers will result in a less than 50% increase in output, sometimes much less (cf. *The Miserable Mathematics of the Man-Month* - `http://paul-m-jones.com/archives/1591`).

Alternatively, we could put the existing developers on the rewrite project, and the new hires on maintenance of the existing program. This too reveals a knowledge problem because the new developers are completely unfamiliar with the system. Where will they get the knowledge they need to do their work? From the existing developers, of course, who will still need to spend valuable time communicating their knowledge to the new hires. Once again, we see that the linear increase in developers leads to a less-than-linear increase in productivity.

The Schedule Problem

To deal with the knowledge problem and the related communication costs, some may feel the best way to handle the project would be to dedicate all the existing developers on the rewrite, and delay maintenance and upgrades on the existing system until the rewrite is done. This is a great temptation because the developers will be all too eager to salve their own pains and become their own customers - becoming excited about what features they want to have and what fixes they want to make. These desires will lead them to overestimate their own ability to perform a full rewrite and underestimate the amount of time needed to complete it. The managers, for their part, will accept the optimism of the developers, perhaps adding some buffer in the schedule for good measure.

The overconfidence and optimism of the developers will morph into frustration and pain when they realize the task is actually much greater and more overwhelming than they first thought. The rewrite will go on much longer than anticipated, not by a little, but by an order of magnitude or more. For the duration of the rewrite, the existing program will languish - buggy and missing features - disappointing existing customers and failing to attract new ones. The rewrite project will, at the end, become a panicked death march to get it done at all costs, and the result will be a codebase that is just as bad as the first one, only in different ways. It will be merely a copy of the first system, because schedule pressures will have dictated that new features be delayed until after an initial release is achieved.

Iterative Refactoring

Given the risks associated with a complete rewrite, I recommend refactoring instead. Refactoring means that the *quality* of the program is improved in small steps, without changing the *functionality* of the program. A single, relatively small change is introduced across the entire system. The system is then tested to make sure it still works properly, and finally, the system is put into production. A second small change builds on the previous one, and so on. Over a period of time, the system becomes markedly easier to maintain and improve.

A refactoring approach is decidedly less appealing than a complete rewrite. It defies the core sensibilities of most developers. The developers have to continue working with the system as it is, warts and all, for long periods of time. They do not get to switch over to the latest, hottest framework. They do not get to become their own customers and indulge their desires to do things right the first time. Being a longer-term strategy, the refactoring approach does not appeal to a culture that values rapid development of new applications over patching existing ones. Developers usually prefer to start their own new projects, not maintain older projects developed by others.

However, as a risk-reducing strategy, using an iterative refactoring approach is undeniably superior to a rewrite. The individual refactorings themselves are small compared to any similar portion of a rewrite project. They can be applied in much shorter periods of time than a comparable feature would be in a rewrite, and they leave the existing codebase in a working state at the end of each iteration. At no point does the existing application stop operating or progressing. The iterative refactorings can be integrated into a larger process with scheduling that allows for cycles of bug fixes, feature additions, and refactorings to improve the next cycle.

Finally, the goal of any single refactoring step is not perfection. The goal in each step is merely improvement. We are not trying to realize an impossible goal over a long period of time. We are taking small steps toward easily-visualized goals that can be accomplished in short timeframes. Each small refactoring win will both improve morale and drive enthusiasm for the next refactoring step. Over time, these many small wins accumulate into a single big win: a fully-modernized codebase that has never stopped generating revenue for the business.

Legacy Frameworks

Until now, we have been discussing legacy applications as page-based, include-oriented systems. However, there is also a large base of legacy code out there using public frameworks.

Framework-based Legacy Applications

Each different public framework in PHP land is its own unique hell. Applications written in *CakePHP* (`http://cakephp.org/`)suffer from different legacy issues than those written in CodeIgniter, Solar, Symfony 1, Zend Framework 1, and so on. Each of these different frameworks, and their varying work-alikes, encourage different kinds of tight-coupling in applications. Thus, the specific steps needed to refactor applications built using one of these frameworks are very different from the steps needed for a different framework.

As such, various parts of this book may be useful as a guide to refactoring different parts of a legacy application based on a public framework, but as a whole, the book is not targeted at refactoring applications based on these public frameworks.

In-house, private, or otherwise non-public frameworks under the direct control of their own architects within the organization likely to benefit from the refactorings included in this book.

Refactoring to a Framework

I sometimes hear about how developers wisely wish to avoid a complete rewrite and instead want to refactor or migrate to a public framework. This sounds like the best of both worlds, combining an iterative approach with the developers' desire to use the hottest new technology.

My experience with legacy PHP applications has been that they are almost as resistant to framework integration as they are to unit testing. If the application was already in a state where its logic could be ported to a framework, there would be little need to port it in the first place.

However, by the time we have completed the refactorings in this book, the application is very likely to be in a state that will be much more amenable to a public framework migration. Whether the developers will still want to do so is another matter.

Review and next steps

At this point, we have realized that a rewrite, while appealing, is a dangerous approach. An iterative refactoring approach sounds a lot more like actual work, but has the benefit of being achievable and realistic.

The next step is to prepare ourselves for the refactoring approach by getting some prerequisites out of the way. After that, we will proceed toward modernizing our legacy application in a series of relatively small steps, one step per chapter with each step broken down into an easy-to-follow process with answers to common questions.

Let's get started!

2
Prerequisites

Before we begin modernizing our application, we need to make sure we have the necessary prerequisites in place to do the work of refactoring. These are as following:

- A revision control system
- A PHP version of 5.0 or higher
- An editor or IDE with multi-file search-and-replace
- A style guide of some sort
- A test suite

Revision control

Revision control (also known as source control or version control) allows us to keep track of the prerequisites:revision control" changes we make to our codebase. We can make a change, then commit it to source control, make more changes and commit them, and push our changes to other developers on the team. If we discover an error, we can revert to an earlier version of the codebase to a point where the error does not exist and start over.

If you are not using a source control tool like Git, Mercurial, Subversion, or some other revision control system, then that's the very first thing you need to put in place. Using source control will be a great benefit to you, even if you don't modernize your PHP application at all.

I prefer Mercurial in many ways, but I recognize that Git is more widely used, and as such I must recommend Git for new users of source control systems.

While it is beyond the scope of this book to discuss how to set up and use a source control system, there are some good Git books and Mercurial books available for free.

PHP version

In order to prerequisites:PHP 5.0" apply the refactorings listed in this book, we need at least PHP 5.0 installed. Yes, I know that PHP 5.0 is ancient, but we are talking about legacy applications here. It is entirely possible that the business owners have not upgraded their PHP versions in years. PHP 5.0 is the bare minimum, because that was when class autoloading became available, and we depend on autoloading as one of our very first improvements. (If for whatever reason we are stuck on PHP 4.x, then this book will be of little use.)

If we can get away with it, we should upgrade to the very latest version of PHP. I recommend using the most-recent version of PHP available to your chosen operating system. At the time of the latest update to this book, the most recent versions were PHP 5.6.11, 5.5.27, and 5.4.43.

Doing an upgrade from an older PHP version might itself entail modifying the application, as there are changes between minor versions in PHP. Approach this with care and attention to detail: check the release notes for the release and all intervening releases, look over the codebase, identify problems, make fixes, spot check locally, commit, push, and notify QA.

Editor/IDE

Throughoutprerequisites:editor/IDE" this book, we will be doing a lot of searching and modifying across the legacy codebase. We will need to have a text editor or IDE that allows us to find and replace text in multiple files at once. These include:

- Emacs
- PHPStorm
- SublimeText
- TextMate
- Vim
- Zend Studio

There are likely to be others as well.

Alternatively, if our CLI-fu is strong, we may wish to use grep and sed at the command line across multiple files at once.

Style Guide

Using a consistent prerequisites:style guide" coding style throughout the codebase is an important consideration. Most legacy codebases that I have seen are a mishmash of styles preferred by the various authors over time. One example of this kind of mishmash is the mixing of tabs and spaces for indenting code blocks: the developers early in the project used 2 spaces for indents, developers in the middle of the project used tabs, and recent developers used 4 spaces. This had the effect of putting some child blocks completely out prerequisites:style guide" of line with their parent blocks, either too much indented or not enough, making it difficult to scan for the beginning or end of a block.

We all long for a consistent, familiar coding style. There are few urges stronger than the urge to reformat an unfamiliar or undesired coding style to one that is more preferable. But modifying the existing style, no matter how ugly or inconsistent it is, can give rise to subtle bugs and behavioral changes from something as simple as adding or removing braces in a conditional. Then again, we want the code to be consistent and familiar so that we can read it with a minimum of cognitive friction.

It is tough to give good advice here. I suggest that the only reason to modify the existing style is when it is inconsistent within an individual file. If it is ugly or unfamiliar but otherwise consistent throughout the codebase, reformatting is likely to cause more problems than it solves.

If you decide to reformat, do so only as you move bits of code from one file to another, or as you move files from one location to another. This combines the large change of extraction-and-relocation with the more subtle change of style modification, and makes it possible to test those changes in a single pass.

Finally, you may want to convert to a completely new style, even though the existing one is consistent throughout the codebase. Resist that urge. If your desire to reformat in toto is overwhelming and cannot be ignored, use a publicly documented non-project-specific coding style instead of trying to create or apply your own personal or project-specific style. The code in this book uses the PSR-1 and PSR-2 style recommendations as a reflection of that advice.

Test suite

As this is a bookprerequisites:test suite" about legacy applications, it would be the height of optimism to expect that the codebase has a suite of unit tests. Most legacy applications, especially include-oriented, page-based applications, are highly resistant to unit tests. There are no units to test, only a spaghetti mess of tightly coupled functionality.

And yet it is possible to test a legacy application. The key here is not to test what the system units ought to do, but what the system as a whole already does. The criteria for a successful test is that the system generates the same output after a change as it did before that change. This kind of test is called a *characterization test*.

It is not in the scope of this book to discuss how to write a characterization test suite. There are some good tools out there already for writing these kinds of tests, such as Selenium and Codeception. Having tests of this sort before we go about refactoring the codebase is invaluable. We will be able to run the tests after each change to make sure the application still operates properly.

I will not pretend prerequisites:test suite" that we are likely to spend the time writing these kinds of tests. If we were interested in testing to begin with, we would have a test suite of some sort already. The issue here is a very human one, not of doing the right thing for its own sake or even of rational expectations but of incentives based on rewards. The reward for writing tests is a longer-term one, whereas making an improvement to the codebase right now feels immediately rewarding, even if we have to suffer with manual checking of the application output.

If you have the time, the self-discipline, and the resources, the best option is to create a series of characterization tests for the parts of the application you know you will be refactoring. It is the most responsible and most professional approach. As a second-best option, if you have a QA team that already has a series of application-wide tests in place, you can delegate the testing process to them since they are doing it anyway. Perhaps they will show you how to run the test suite locally as you make changes to the codebase. Finally, as the least-professional but most-likely option, you will have to pseudo-test or spot check the application by hand when you make changes. This is probably what you are used to doing anyway. As your codebase improves, the reward for improving your own practices will become more evident; as with refactoring in general, the goal is to make things better than they were before in small increments, not to insist on immediate perfection.

Review and next steps

At this point we should have all our prerequisites in place, especially our revision control system and a modern version of PHP. Now we can begin with our very first step in refactoring: adding an autoloader to the codebase.

3
Implement an Autoloader

In this step, we will set up automatic class loading. After this, when we need a class file, we will not need an `include` or `require` statement to load it for us. You should review the PHP documentation on autoloaders before continuing – `http://www.php.net/manual/en/language.oop5.autoload.php`.

PSR-0

There are many different autoloader recommendations in PHP land. The one we will be using to modernize our legacy application is based on something called `PSR-0`.

PSR-0 is a PHP Framework Interoperability Group recommendation for structuring your class files. The recommendation rises out of a long history of projects using the "class-to-file" naming convention from the days of PHP 4. Originating with Horde and PEAR, the convention was adopted by early PHP 5 projects such as Solar and Zend Framework, and later by projects such as Symfony2.

We use PSR-0 instead of the newer PSR-4 recommendation because we are dealing with legacy code, code that was probably developed before PHP 5.3 namespaces came into being. Code written before PHP 5.3 did not have access to namespace separators, so authors following the class-to-file naming convention would typically use underscores in class names as a pseudo-namespace separator. PSR-0 makes an allowance for older non-PHP-5.3 pseudo-namespaces, making it more suitable for our legacy needs, whereas PSR-4 does not.

Under PSR-0, the class name maps directly to a file system sub-path. Given a fully-qualified class name, any PHP 5.3 namespace separators are converted to directory separators, and underscores in the class portion of the name are also converted to directory separators. (Underscores in the namespace portion proper are *not* converted to directory separators.) The result is prefixed with a base directory location, and suffixed with .php, to create a file path where the class file may be found. For example, the fully-qualified class name \Foo\Bar\Baz_Dib would be found in a sub-path named Foo/Bar/Baz/Dib.php on a UNIX-style file system.

A Single Location for Classes

Before we implement a PSR-0 autoloader, we need to pick a directory location in the codebase to hold every class that will ever be used in the codebase. Some projects already have such a location; it may be called includes, classes, src, lib or something similar.

If a location like that already exists, examine it carefully. Does it have *only* class files in it, or is it a combination of class files and other kinds of files? If it has anything besides class files in it, or if no such location exists, create a new directory location and call it classes (or some other properly descriptive name).

This directory will be the central location for all classes used throughout the project. Later, we will begin moving classes from their scattered locations in the project to this central location.

Add Autoloader Code

Once we have a central directory location for our class files, we need to set up an autoloader to look in that location for classes. We can create the autoloader as a static method, an instance method, an anonymous function, or a regular global function. (Which one we use is not as important as actually doing the autoloading.) Then we will register it with spl_autoload_register() early in our bootstrap or setup code, before any classes are called.

As a Global Function

Perhaps the most straightforward way to implement our new autoloader code is as a global function. Below, we find the autoloader code to use; the function name is prefixed with mlaphp_ to make sure it does not conflict with any existing function names.

setup.php
```
1  <?php
```

```
2 // ... setup code ...
3
4 // define an autoloader function in the global namespace
5 function mlaphp_autoloader($class)
6 {
7 // strip off any leading namespace separator from PHP 5.3
8 $class = ltrim($class, '\\');
9
10 // the eventual file path
11 $subpath = '';
12
13 // is there a PHP 5.3 namespace separator?
14 $pos = strrpos($class, '\\');
15 if ($pos !== false) {
16 // convert namespace separators to directory separators
17 $ns = substr($class, 0, $pos);
18 $subpath = str_replace('\\', DIRECTORY_SEPARATOR, $ns)
19 . DIRECTORY_SEPARATOR;
20 // remove the namespace portion from the final class name portion
21 $class = substr($class, $pos + 1);
22 }
23
24 // convert underscores in the class name to directory separators
25 $subpath .= str_replace('_', DIRECTORY_SEPARATOR, $class);
26
27 // the path to our central class directory location
28 $dir = '/path/to/app/classes';
29
30 // prefix with the central directory location and suffix with .php,
31 // then require it.
32 $file = $dir . DIRECTORY_SEPARATOR . $subpath . '.php';
33 require $file;
34 }
35
36 // register it with SPL
37 spl_autoload_register('mlaphp_autoloader');
38 ?>
```

Note that the `$dir` variable represents an absolute directory as the base path for our central class directory. As an alternative on PHP 5.3 and later, it is perfectly acceptable to use the `__DIR__` constant in that variable so the absolute path is no longer hard-coded, but is instead relative to the file where the function is located. For example:

```
1 <?php
2 // go "up one directory" for the central classes location
3 $dir = dirname(__DIR__) . '/classes';
4 ?>
```

If you are stuck on PHP 5.2 for some reason, the `__DIR__` constant is not available. You can replace `dirname(__DIR__)` with `dirname(dirname(__FILE__))` in that case.

As a Closure

If we are using PHP 5.3, we can create the autoloader code as a closure and register it with SPL in a single step:

```
setup.php
1 <?php
2 // ... setup code ...
3
4 // register an autoloader as an anonymous function
5 spl_autoload_register(function ($class) {
6 // ... the same code as in the global function ...
7 });
8
9 // ... other setup code ...
10 ?>
```

As a Static or Instance method

This is my preferred way of setting up an autoloader. Instead of using a function, we create the autoloader code in a class as an instance method or a static method. I recommend instance methods over static ones, but your situation will dictate which is more appropriate.

First, we create our autoloader class file in our central class directory location. If we are using PHP 5.3 or later, we should use a proper namespace; otherwise, we use underscores as pseudo-namespace separators.

The following is a PHP 5.3 example. Under versions earlier than PHP 5.3, we would omit the `namespace` declaration and name the class `Mlaphp_Autoloader`. Either way, the file should be in the sub-path `Mlaphp/Autoloader.php`:

/path/to/app/classes/Mlaphp/Autoloader.php

```
1  <?php
2  namespace Mlaphp;
3
4  class Autoloader
5  {
6  // an instance method alternative
7  public function load($class)
8  {
9  // ... the same code as in the global function ...
10 }
11
12 // a static method alternative
13 static public function loadStatic($class)
14 {
15 // ... the same code as in the global function ...
16 }
17 }
18 ?>
```

Then, in the setup or bootstrap file, `require_once` the class file, instantiate it if needed, and register the method with SPL. Note that we use the array-callable format here, where the first array element is either a class name or an object instance, and the second element is the method to call:

setup.php

```
1  <?php
2  // ... setup code ...
3
4  // require the autoloader class file
5  require_once '/path/to/app/classes/Mlaphp/Autoloader.php';
6
7  // STATIC OPTION: register a static method with SPL
8  spl_autoload_register(array('Mlaphp\Autoloader', 'loadStatic'));
9
10 // INSTANCE OPTION: create the instance and register the method
with SPL
11 $autoloader = new \Mlaphp\Autoloader();
12 spl_autoload_register(array($autoloader, 'load'));
13
14 // ... other setup code ...
15 ?>
```

Please pick either an instance method or a static method, not both. The one is not a fallback for the other.

Using The __autoload() Function

If we are stuck on PHP 5.0 for some reason, we can use the __autoload() function in place of the SPL autoloader registry. There are drawbacks to doing things this way, but under PHP 5.0 it is our only alternative. We do not need to register it with SPL (in fact, we cannot, since SPL was not introduced until PHP 5.1). We will not be able to mix-and-match other autoloaders in this implementation; only one __autoload() function is allowed. If an __autoload() function is already defined, we will need to merge this code with any code already existing in the function:

```
setup.php
1 <?php
2 // ... setup code ...
3
4 // define an __autoload() function
5 function __autoload($class)
6 {
7 // ... the global function code ...
8 }
9
10 // ... other setup code ...
11 ?>
```

I strongly recommend against using this kind of implementation in PHP 5.1 and later.

Autoloader Priority

Regardless of how we implement our autoloader code, we need it to be available *before* any classes get called in the codebase. It cannot hurt to register the autoloader as one of the very first bits of logic in our codebase, probably in a setup or bootstrap script.

Common Questions

What If I Already Have An Autoloader?

Some legacy applications may already have a custom autoloader in place. If this is our situation, we have some options:

1. **Use the existing autoloader as-is**: This is our best option if there is already a central directory location for the application class files.

2. **Modify the existing autoloader to add PSR-0 behavior**: This is a good option if the autoloader does not conform to PSR-0 recommendations.

3. Register the PSR-0 autoloader described in this chapter with SPL in addition to the existing autoloader. This is another good option when the existing autoloader does not conform to PSR-0 recommendations.

Other legacy codebases may have a third-party autoloader in place, such as Composer. If Composer is present, we can obtain its autoloader instance and add our central class directory location for autoloading like so:

```php
1 <?php
2 // get the registered Composer autoloader instance from the vendor/
3 // subdirectory
4 $loader = require '/path/to/app/vendor/autoload.php';
5
6 // add our central class directory location; do not use a class
prefix as
7 // we may have more than one top-level namespace in the central
location
8 $loader->add('', '/path/to/app/classes');
9 ?>
```

With that, we can co-opt Composer for our own purposes, making our own autoloader code unnecessary.

What are the Performance Implications Of Autoloading?

There is some reason to think that using autoloaders may cause a slight performance drag compared to using `include`, but the evidence is mixed and situation-dependent. If it is true that autoloading is comparatively slower, how big of a performance hit can be expected?

I assert that, when modernizing a legacy application, it is probably not an important consideration. Any performance drag incurred from autoloading is minuscule compared to the other possible performance issues in your legacy application, such as the database interactions.

In most legacy applications, or even in most modern ones, attempting to optimize performance on autoloading is a case of attempting to optimize on the wrong resource. There are other resources that are likely to be worse offenders, just ones that we don't see or don't think of.

If autoloading is the single worst performance bottleneck in your legacy application, then you are in fantastic shape. (In that case, you should return this book for a refund, and then tell me if you are hiring, because I want to work for you.)

How Do Class Names Map To File Names?

The PSR-0 rules can be confusing. Here are some class-to-file mapping examples to illustrate its expectations:

```
Foo             => Foo.php
Foo_Bar         => Foo/Bar.php
Foo             => Foo/Bar.php
Foo_Bar\Bar     => Foo_Bar/Baz.php
Foo\Bar\Baz     => Foo/Bar/Baz.php # ???
Foo\Baz_Bar     => Foo/Bar/Baz.php # ???
Foo_Bar_Baz     => Foo/Bar/Baz.php # ???
```

We can see that there is some unexpected behavior in the last three examples. This is born of the transitional nature of PSR-0: `Foo\Bar\Baz`, `Foo\Bar_Baz`, and `Foo_Bar_Baz` all map to the same file. Why is this?

Recall that pre-PHP-5.3 codebases did not have namespaces, and so used underscores as a pseudo-namespace separator. PHP 5.3 introduced a real namespace separator. The PSR-0 standard had to accommodate both cases simultaneously, so it honors underscores in the relative class name (i.e., the final part of the fully-qualified name) as directory separators, but underscores in the namespace part are left alone.

The lesson here is that if you are on PHP 5.3, you should never use underscores in your relative class names (although underscores in the namespace are fine). If you are on a version before PHP 5.3, you have no choice but to use only underscores, as there is only the class name and no actual namespace portion; interpret underscores as namespace separators in that case.

Review and next steps

At this point we have not modified our legacy application very much. We have added and registered some autoloader code, but it is not actually being called yet.

No matter. Having an autoloader is critical to the next step in modernizing our legacy application. Using an autoloader will allow us to start removing `include` statements that only load classes and functions. The remaining `include` statements will be logical-flow includes, showing us which parts of the system are logic and which are definition-only. This is the beginning of our transition from an include-oriented architecture toward a class-oriented architecture.

4
Consolidate Classes and Functions

Now that we have an autoloader in place, we can begin to remove all the `include` calls that only load up class and function definitions. When we are done, the only remaining `include` calls will be those that are executing logic. This will make it easier to see which `include` calls are forming the logic paths in our legacy application, and which are merely providing definitions.

We will start with a scenario where the codebase is structured relatively well. Afterwards, we will answer some questions related to layouts that are not so amenable to revision.

> For the purposes of this chapter, we will use the term `include` to cover not just `include` but also `require`, `include_once`, and `require_once`.

Consolidate Class Files

First, we will consolidate all the application classes to our central directory location as determined in the previous chapter. Doing so will put them where our autoloader can find them. Here is the general process we will follow:

1. Find an `include` statement that pulls in a class definition file.
2. Move that class definition file to our central class directory location, making sure that it is placed in a sub-path matching the PSR-0 rules.
3. In the original file *and in all other files in the codebase* where an `include` pulls in that class definition, remove that `include` statement.

4. Spot check to make sure that all the files now autoload that class by browsing to them or otherwise running them.

5. Commit, push, and notify QA.

6. Repeat until there are no more `include` calls that pull in class definitions.

For our examples, we will assume we have a legacy application with this partial file system layout:

/path/to/app/

```
classes/            # our central class directory location
Mlaphp/
Autoloader.php      # A hypothetical autoloader class
foo/ bar/ baz.php   # a page script
includes/           # a common "includes" directory
setup.php           # setup code
index.php           # a page script
lib/                # a directory with some classes in it
sub/ Auth.php       # class Auth { ... }
Role.php            # class Role { ... }
User.php            # class User { ... }
```

Your own legacy application may not match this exactly, but you get the idea.

Find a candidate include

We begin by picking a file, any file, then we examine it for `include` calls. The code therein might look like this:

```
1 <?php
2 require 'includes/setup.php';
3 require_once 'lib/sub/User.php';
4
5 // ...
6 $user = new User();
7 // ...
8 ?>
```

We can see that there is a new `User` class being instantiated. On inspecting the `lib/sub/User.php` file, we can see it is the only class defined therein.

Move the class file

Having identified an `include` statement that loads a class definition, we now move that class definition file to the central class directory location so that our autoloader function can find it. The resulting file system layout now looks like this (note that `User.php` is now in `classes/`):

```
/path/to/app/
classes/                      # our central class directory location
Mlaphp/ Autoloader.php        # A hypothetical autoloader class
User.php                      # class User { ... }
foo/ bar/ baz.php             # a page script
includes/                     # a common "includes" directory
setup.php                     # setup code
db_functions.php              # a function definition file
index.php                     # a page script
lib/                          # a directory with some classes in it
sub/
Auth.php                      # class Auth { ... }
Role.php                      # class Role { ... } ~~
```

Remove the related include calls

Now the problem is that our original file is trying to `include` the class file from its old location, a location that no longer exists. We need to remove that call from the code:

index.php
```
1 <?php
2 require 'includes/setup.php';
3
4 // ...
5 // the User class is now autoloaded
6 $user = new User();
7 // ...
8 ?>
```

However, there are likely to be other places where the code attempts to load the now-missing `lib/sub/User.php` file.

This is where a project-wide search facility comes in handy. We have different options here, depending on your editor/IDE of choice and operating system.

- In GUI editors like TextMate, SublimeText, and PHPStorm, there is usually a **Find in Project** menu item that we can use to search for a string or regular expression across all the application files at once.

- In other editors like Emacs and Vim, there is generally a key-binding that will search all the files in a particular directory and its subdirectories for a string or regular expression.

- Finally, if you are of the old school, you can use `grep` at the command line to search all the files in a particular directory and its subdirectories.

The point is to find all the `include` calls that refer to `lib/sub/User.php`. Because the `include` calls can be formed in different ways, we need to use a regular expression like this to search for the `include` calls:

```
^[ \t]*(include|include_once|require|require_once).*User\.php
```

If you are not familiar with regular expressions, here is a breakdown of what we are looking for:

```
^                  Starting at the beginning of each line,
[ \t]*             followed by zero or more spaces and/or tabs,
(include|...)      followed by any of these words,
.*                 followed by any characters at all,
User\.php          followed by User.php, and we don't care what comes
after.
```

(Regular expressions use . to mean `any character` so we have to specify `User\.php` to indicate we mean a literal dot, not any character.)

If we use a regular expression search to find those strings in the legacy codebase, we will be presented with a list of all matching lines and their corresponding files. Unfortunately, it is up to us to examine each line to see if it really is a reference to the `lib/sub/User.php` file. For example, this line might turn up in the search results:

```
include_once("/usr/local/php/lib/User.php");
```

However, clearly it is not the `User.php` file we are looking for.

We could be more strict with our regular expression so that we search specifically for `lib/sub/User.php` but that is more likely to miss some `include` calls, especially those in files under the `lib/` or `sub/` directories. For example, an `include` in a file in `sub/` could look like this:

```
include 'User.php';
```

As such, it's better to be a little loose with the search to get every possible candidate, then work through the results manually.

Examine each search result line, and if it is an `include` that pulls in the `User` class, remove it and save the file. Keep a list of each modified file, as we will need to test them later.

At the end of this, we will have removed all the `include` calls for that class throughout the codebase.

Spot check the codebase

After removing the `include` statements for the given class, we now need to make sure the application works. Unfortunately, because we have no testing process in place, this means we need to pseudo-test or spot check by browsing to or otherwise invoking the modified files. In practice this is generally not difficult, but it is tedious.

When we spot check we are looking specifically for *file not found* and *class not defined* errors. These mean, respectively, that a file tried to `include` the missing class file, or that the autoloader failed to find the class file.

To do the testing we need to set PHP error reporting so that it either shows us the errors directly, or logs the errors to a file that we examine while testing the codebase. In addition, the error reporting level needs to be sufficiently strict that we actually see the errors. In general, `error_reporting(E_ALL)` is what we want, but because this is a legacy codebase, it may show more errors than we can bear (especially *variable not defined* notices). As such, it may be more productive to set `error_reporting(E_WARNING)`. The error reporting values can be set either in a setup or bootstrap file, or in the correct `php.ini` file.

Commit, Push, Notify QA

After the testing is complete and all errors have been fixed, commit the code to source control and (if needed) push it to the central code repository. If you have a QA team, now would be the time to notify them that a new testing round is needed, and provide them the list of files to test.

Do ... While

That is the process to convert a single class from `include` to autoloading. Go back through the codebase and find the next `include` that pulls in a class file and begin the process again. Continue doing so until all classes have been consolidated into the central class directory location and their relevant `include` lines have been removed. Yes, this is a tedious, tiresome, and time-consuming process, but it is a necessary step towards modernizing our legacy codebase.

Consolidate functions into class files

Not all legacy applications use a large set of classes. Often, instead of classes, there is a significant number of user-defined functions for core logic.

Using functions is not a problem in itself, but it does mean that we need to `include` the files where the functions are defined. But autoloading only works for classes. It would be good to find a way to automatically load the function files as well as the class files. That would help us remove even more `include` calls.

The solution here is to move the functions into class files, and call the functions as static methods on those classes. That way, the autoloader can load up the class file for us, and then we can call the methods in that class.

This procedure is more complex than when we consolidated class files. Here is the general process we will follow:

1. Find an `include` statement that pulls in a function definition file.
2. Convert that function definition file into a class file of static methods; we need to pick a unique name for the class, and we may need to rename the functions to more suitable method names.
3. In the original file *and in all other files in the codebase* where any functions from that file are used, change calls to those functions into static method calls.
4. Spot check to see if the new static method calls work by browsing to or otherwise invoking the affected files.
5. Move the class file to the central class directory location.
6. In the original file *and in all other files in the codebase* where an `include` pulls in that class definition, remove the relevant `include` statement.
7. Spot check again to make sure that all the files now autoload that class by browsing to them or otherwise running them.

8. Commit, push, and notify QA.
9. Repeat until there are no more `include` calls that pull in function definition files.

Find a candidate include

We pick a file, any file, and look through it for `include` calls. The code in our chosen file might look like this:

```php
1 <?php
2 require 'includes/setup.php';
3 require_once 'includes/db_functions.php';
4
5 // ...
6 $result = db_query('SELECT * FROM table_name');
7 // ...
8 ?>
```

We can see that there is a `db_query()` function being used, and on inspecting the `includes/db_functions.php` file, we can see that function along with several others defined therein.

Convert the function file to a class file

Let's say that the `db_functions.php` file looks something like this:

includes/db_functions.php
```php
1 <?php
2 function db_query($query_string)
3 {
4 // ... code to perform a query ...
5 }
6
7 function db_get_row($query_string)
8 {
9 // ... code to get the first result row
10 }
11
12 function db_get_col($query_string)
13 {
14 // ... code to get the first column of results ...
15 }
16 ?>
```

To convert this function file to a class file, we need to pick a unique name for the class we're about to create. It seems pretty clear in this case, both from the file name and from the function names, that these are all database-related calls. As such, we'll call this class Db.

Now that we have a name, we'll create the class. The functions will become static methods in the class. We are not going to move the file just yet; leave it in place with its current file name.

Then we make our changes to convert the file to a class definition. If we change function names, we need to keep a list of old and the new names for later use. After the changes, it will look something like the following (note the changed method names):

```
includes/db_functions.php
1  <?php
2  class Db
3  {
4  public static function query($query_string)
5  {
6  // ... code to perform a query ...
7  }
8
9  public static function getRow($query_string)
10 {
11 // ... code to get the first result row
12 }
13
14 public static function getCol($query_string)
15 {
16 // ... code to get the first column of results ...
17 }
18 }
19 ?>
```

The changes are very moderate: we wrapped the functions in a unique class name, marked them as `public static`, and made minor changes to the function names. We made no changes at all to the function signatures or code in the functions themselves.

Change function calls to static method calls

We have converted the contents of `db_functions.php` from function definitions to a class definition. If we try to run the application now, it will fail with "undefined function" errors. So, the next step is to find all of the relevant function calls throughout the application and rename them to static method calls on our new class.

There is no easy way to do this. This is another case where project-wide search-and-replace becomes very handy. Using our preferred project-wide search tool, search for the `old` function call, and replace it with the `new` static method call. For example, using a regular expression, we might do this:

Search for:

```
db_query\s*\(
```

Replace with:

```
Db::query(
```

The regular expression indicates the opening parenthesis, not the closing one, as we don't need to look for parameters in the function call. This helps to distinguish from function names that might be prefixed with the function name we're searching for, such as `db_query_raw()`. The regular expression also allows for optional whitespace between the function name and the opening parenthesis, since some style guides recommend such spacing.

Perform this search-and-replace for each of the `old` function names in the old function file, converting each to the `new` static method call in the new class file.

Spot check the static method calls

When we are finished renaming the old function names to the new static method calls, we need to run through the codebase to make sure everything works. Again, there is no easy way to do this. You may need to go so far as browsing to, or otherwise invoking, each file that was changed in this process.

Move the class file

At this point we have replaced the contents of the function definition file with a class definition, and "testing" has showed that the new static method calls work as expected. Now we need to move the file to our central class directory location and name it properly.

Currently, our class definition is in the `includes/db_functions.php` file. The class in that file is named `Db`, so move the file to its new autoloadable location as `classes/Db.php`. Afterwards, the file system will look something like this:

```
/path/to/app/
classes/          # our central class directory location
Db.php            # class Db { ... }
Mlaphp/
Autoloader.php    # A hypothetical autoloader class
```

```
User.php              # class User { ... }
foo/
bar/
baz.php               # a page script
includes/             # a common "includes" directory
setup.php             # setup code
index.php             # a page script
lib/                  # a directory with some classes in it
sub/
Auth.php              # class Auth { ... }
Role.php              # class Role { ... }
```

Do ... While

Finally, we follow the same ending process as we did when moving class files:

- Remove the related `include` calls for the function definition file throughout the codebase
- Spot check the codebase
- Commit, push, notify QA

Now repeat it for every function definition file we find in the codebase.

Common Questions

Should we remove the autoloader include call?

If we placed our autoloader code in a class as a static or instance method, our search for `include` calls will reveal the inclusion of that class file. If you remove that `include` call, autoloading will fail, because the class file will not have been loaded. This is a chicken-and-egg problem. The solution is to leave the autoloader `include` in place as part of our bootstrapping or setup code. If we are fully diligent about removing `include` calls, that is likely to be the only `include` remaining in the codebase.

How should we pick files for candidate include calls?

There are several ways to go about this. We could do the following:

- We can manually traverse the entire codebase and work file-by-file.
- We can generate a list of class and function definition files, and then generate a list of files that `include` those files.
- We can search for every `include` call and look at the related file to see if it has class or function definitions.

What if an include defines more than one class?

Sometime a class definition file may have more than one class definition in it. This can mess with the autoloading process. If a file named `Foo.php` defines both `Foo` and `Bar` classes, then the `Bar` class will never be autoloaded, because the file name is wrong.

The solution is to split the single file into multiple files. That is, create one file per class, and name each file for the class it contains per the PSR-0 naming and autoloading expectations.

What if the one-class-per-file rule is disagreeable?

I sometimes hear complaints about how the one-class-per-file rules is somehow wasteful or otherwise not aesthetically pleasing when examining the file system. Isn't it a drag on performance to load that many files? What if some classes are only needed along with some other class, such as an `Exception` that is only used in one place? I have some responses here:

- There is, of course, a performance reduction in loading two files instead of one. The question is *how much* of a reduction, and *compared to what*? I assert that, compared to the other more likely performance issues in our legacy application, the drag from loading multiple files is a rounding error. It is more likely that we have other, far greater performance concerns. If it really is a problem, using a bytecode cache like APC will reduce or completely remove these comparatively small performance hits.

- Consistency, consistency, consistency. If some of the time a class file has only one class in it, and at other times a class file has more than one class in it, that inconsistency will later become a source of cognitive friction for everyone on the project. One of the main themes through legacy applications is that of inconsistency; let us reduce that inconsistency as much as we can by adhering to the one-class-per-file rule.

If we feel that some classes naturally belong together, it is perfectly acceptable to place the subordinate or child classes in a subdirectory beneath the master or parent class. The subdirectory should be named for that higher class or namespace, per the PSR-0 naming rules.

For example, if we have a series of `Exception` classes related to a `Foo` class:

```
Foo.php                          # class Foo { ... }
Foo/
NotFoundException.php            # class Foo_NotFoundException { ... }
MalformedDataException.php       # class Foo_MalformedDataException { ...
}
```

Renaming classes in this way will change the related class names throughout the codebase where they are instantiated or otherwise referenced.

What if a Class or Function is defined inline?

I have seen cases where a page script has one or more classes or functions defined inside it, generally when the classes or functions are used only by that particular page script.

In these cases, remove the class definitions from the script and place them in their own files in the central class directory location. Be sure to name the files for their class names per the PSR-0 autoloader rules. Similarly, move the function definitions to their own related class file as static methods, and rename the function calls to static method calls.

What if a definition file also executes logic?

I have also seen the opposite case, where a class file has some logic that gets executed as a result of the file being loaded. For example, a class definition file might look like this:

/path/to/foo.php
```
1 <?php
2 echo "Doing something here ...";
```

```
3 log_to_file('a log entry');
4 db_query('UPDATE table_name SET incrementor = incrementor + 1');
5
6 class Foo
7 {
8 // the class
9 }
10 ?>
```

In the above case, the logic before the class definition will be executed when the file is loaded, even if the class is never instantiated or otherwise called.

This is a much tougher situation to deal with than when classes are defined inline with a page script. The class should be loadable without side effects, and the other logic should be executable without having to load the class.

In general, the easiest way to deal with this is to modify our relocation process. Cut the class definition from the original file and place it in its own file in the central class directory location. Leave the original file with its executable code in place, and leave all the related `include` calls in place as well. This allows us to pull out the class definition so it can be autoloaded, but scripts that `include` the original file still get the executable behavior.

For example, given the above combined executable code and class definition, we could end up with these two files:

/path/to/foo.php
```
1 <?php
2 echo "Doing something here ...";
3 log_to_file('a log entry');
4 db_query('UPDATE table_name SET incrementor = incrementor + 1');
5 ?>
```

/path/to/app/classes/Foo.php
```
1 <?php
2 class Foo
3 {
4 // the class
5 }
6 ?>
```

This is messy, but it preserves the existing application behavior while allowing for autoloading.

What if two classes have the same name?

When we start moving classes around, we may discover that `application flow A` uses a `Foo` class, and that `application flow B` also uses a `Foo` class, but the two classes of the same name are actually different classes defined in different files. They never conflict with each other because the two different application flows never intersect.

In this case, we have to rename one or both of the classes when we move them to our central class directory location. For example, call one of them `FooOne` and the other `FooTwo`, or pick better descriptive names of your own. Place them each in separate class files named for their class names, per the PSR-0 autoloading rules, and rename all references to these classes throughout the codebase.

What about third-party libraries?

When we consolidate our classes and functions, we may find some third-party libraries in the legacy application. We don't want to move or rename the classes and functions in a third-party library, because that would make it too difficult to upgrade the library later. We would have to remember what classes were moved where and which functions were renamed to what.

With any luck, the third-party library uses autoloading of some sort already. If it comes with its own autoloader, we can add that autoloader to the SPL autoloader registry stack in our setup or bootstrap code. If its autoloading is managed by another autoloader system, such as that found in Composer, we can add *that* autoloader to the SPL autoloader registry stack, again in our setup or bootstrap code.

If the third-party library does not use autoloading, and depends on `include` calls both in its own code and in the legacy application, we are in a bit of a bind. We don't want to modify the code in the library, but at the same time we want to remove `include` calls from the legacy application. The two solutions here are *least-worst* options:

- Modify our application's main autoloader to allow for one or more third party libraries
- Write an additional autoloader for the third-party library and add it to the SPL autoloader registry stack.

Both of these options are beyond the scope of this book. You will need to examine the library in question, determine its class naming scheme, and come up with appropriate autoloader code on your own.

Finally, in terms of how to organize third-party libraries in the legacy application, it might be wise to consolidate them all to their own central location in the codebase. For example, this might be under a directory called 3rdparty/ or external_libs/. If we move a library, we should move the entire package, not just its class files, so we can upgrade it properly later. This will also allow us to exclude the central third-party directory from our search for include calls so that we don't get extra search results from files that we don't want to modify.

What about system-wide libraries?

System-wide library collections, like those provided by Horde and PEAR, are a special case of third-party libraries. They are generally located on the server file system *outside* of the legacy application so they can be available to all applications running on that server. The include statements related to these system-wide libraries generally depend on the include_path settings, or else are referenced by absolute path.

These present a special problem when trying to eliminate include calls that only pull in class and function definitions. If we are lucky enough to be using PEAR-installed libraries, we can modify our existing autoloader to look in two directories instead of one. This is because the PSR-0 naming conventions rise out of the Horde/PEAR conventions. The trailing autoloader code changes from this:

```
1 <?php
2 // convert underscores in the class name to directory separators
3 $subpath .= str_replace('_', DIRECTORY_SEPARATOR, $class);
4
5 // the path to our central class directory location
6 $dir = '/path/to/app/classes'
7
8 // prefix with the central directory location and suffix with .php,
9 // then require it.
10 require $dir . DIRECTORY_SEPARATOR . $subpath . '.php';
11 ?>
```

To this:

```
1 <?php
2 // convert underscores in the class name to directory separators
3 $subpath .= str_replace('_', DIRECTORY_SEPARATOR, $class);
4
5 // the paths to our central class directory location and to PEAR
6 $dirs = array('/path/to/app/classes', '/usr/local/pear/php');
7 foreach ($dirs as $dir) {
```

```
8 $file = $dir . DIRECTORY_SEPARATOR . $subpath . '.php';
9 if (file_exists($file)) {
10 require $file;
11 }
12 }
13 ?>
```

For functions, can we use instance methods instead of static methods?

When we consolidated user-defined global functions into classes, we redefined them as static methods. This left their global scope unchanged. If we feel particularly diligent, we can change them from static to instance methods. This involves more work, but in the end it can make testing easier and is a cleaner technical approach. Given our earlier Db example, using instance instead of static methods would look like this:

classes/Db.php
```
1 <?php
2 class Db
3 {
4 public function query($query_string)
5 {
6 // ... code to perform a query ...
7 }
8
9 public function getRow($query_string)
10 {
11 // ... code to get the first result row
12 }
13
14 public function getCol($query_string)
15 {
16 // ... code to get the first column of results ...
17 }
18 }
19 ?>
```

The only added step when using instance methods instead of static ones is that we need to instantiate the class before calling its methods. That is, instead of this:

```
1 <?php
2 Db::query(...);
3 ?>
```

We would do this:

```
1 <?php
2 $db = new Db();
3 $db->query(...);
4 ?>
```

Even though it is more work in the beginning, I recommend instance methods over static ones. Among other things, it gives us a constructor method that can be called on instantiation, and it makes testing easier in many cases.

If you like, you may wish to start by converting to static methods, and then later convert the static methods to instance methods, along with all the related method calls. However, your schedule and preferences will dictate which approach you choose.

Can we automate this process?

As I have noted before, this is a tedious, tiresome, and time-consuming process. Depending on the size of the codebase, it may take days or weeks of effort to fully consolidate the classes and functions for autoloading. It would be great if there was some way to automate the process to make it both faster and more reliable.

Unfortunately, I have not yet discovered any tools that make this process easier. As far as I can tell, this kind of refactoring is still best done by hand with strong attention to detail. Having obsessive tendencies and long periods of uninterrupted concentration on this task are likely to be of benefit here.

Review and next steps

At this point, we have made a big step forward in modernizing our legacy application. We have begun converting from an *include-oriented* architecture to a *class-oriented* one. Even if we later discover a class or function that we missed, that's OK; we can follow the above process as many times as needed until all definitions have been moved to the central location.

We may still have lots of `include` statements in the application, but those that remain are related to the application flow, and not to pulling in class and function definitions. Any `include` calls that remain are executing logic. We can now see the flow of the application much better.

We have put in place a structure for new functionality. Any time we need to add a new behavior, we can place it in a new class, and that class will be autoloaded whenever we need it. We can stop writing new stand-alone functions; instead, we will write new methods on classes. These new methods will be much more amenable to unit tests.

However, the *existing* classes that we have consolidated for autoloading are likely to have globals and other dependencies in them. This makes them tightly bound to each other and difficult to write tests for. With that in mind, the next step is to examine the dependencies in our existing classes, and attempt to break those dependencies to improve the maintainability of our application.

5

Replace global With Dependency Injection

At this point, all of our classes and functions have been consolidated to a central location, and all related `include` statements have been removed. We would prefer to start writing tests for our classes, but it is very likely that we have a lot of `global` variables embedded in them. These can cause a lot of trouble via action at a distance where modifying a `global` in one place changes its value in another place. The next step, then, is to remove all uses of the `global` keyword from our classes, and inject the necessary dependencies instead.

What Is Dependency Injection?

Dependency injection means that we push our dependencies into a class from the outside, instead of pulling them into a class while inside the class. (U sing `global` pulls a variable into the current scope from the global scope, so it is the opposite of injection.) Dependency injection turns out to be very straightforward as a concept, but is sometimes difficult to adhere to as a discipline.

Global Dependencies

To start with a naive example, let's say an `Example` class needs a database connection. Here we create the connection inside a class method:

classes/Example.php

```php
1 <?php
2 class Example
3 {
4 public function fetch()
```

```
 5 {
 6 $db = new Db('hostname', 'username', 'password');
 7 return $db->query(...);
 8 }
 9 }
10 ?>
```

We are creating the `Db` dependency inside the method that needs it. There are several problems with this. Some of them are:

- Every time we call this method, we create a new database connection, which may strain our resources.
- If we ever need to change the connection parameters, we need to modify them in every place we create a connection.
- It is difficult to see from the outside of this class what its dependencies are.

After writing code like this, many developers discover the `global` keyword, and realize they can create the connection once in a setup file, then pull it in from the global scope:

setup.php
```
1 <?php
2 // some setup code, then:
3 $db = new Db('hostname', 'username', 'password');
4 ?>
```

classes/Example.php
```
1 <?php
2 class Example
3 {
4 public function fetch()
5 {
6 global $db;
7 return $db->query(...);
8 }
9 }
10 ?>
```

Even though we are still pulling in the dependency, this technique solves the problem of multiple database connections using up limited resources, since the same database connection is reused across the codebase. The technique also makes it possible to change our connection parameters in a single location, the setup.php file, instead of several locations. However, one problem remains, and one is added:

- We still cannot see from the outside of the class what its dependencies are.
- If the $db variable is ever changed by any of the calling code, that change is reflected throughout the codebase, leading to debugging trouble.

The last point is a killer. If a method ever sets $db = 'busted'; then the $db value is now a string, and not a database connection object, throughout the entire codebase. Likewise, if the $db object is modified, then it is modified for the entire codebase. This can lead to very difficult debugging sessions.

The replacement process

Thus, we want to remove all global calls from the codebase to make it easier to troubleshoot, and to reveal the dependencies in our classes. Here is the general process we will use to replace global calls with dependency injection:

1. Find a global variable in one of our classes.
2. Move all global variables in that class to the constructor and retain their values as properties, and use the properties instead of the globals.
3. Spot check that the class still works.
4. Convert the global calls in the constructor to constructor parameters.
5. Convert all instantiations of the class to pass the dependencies.
6. Spot check, commit, push, and notify QA.
7. Repeat with the next global call in our class files, until none remain.

In this process, we work *one class at a time* and not *one variable at a time*. The former is much less time-consuming and more unit-oriented than the latter.

Find a global variable

This is easy with a project-wide search function. We search for `global` within the central class directory location, and get back a list of class files with that keyword in them.

Convert global variables to properties

Let's say that our search revealed an `Example` class with code something like the following:

classes/Example.php

```
1 <?php
2 class Example
3 {
4 public function fetch()
5 {
6 global $db;
7 return $db->query(...);
8 }
9 }
10 ?>
```

We now move the global variable to a property that gets set in the constructor, and convert the `fetch()` method to use the property:

classes/Example.php

```
1 <?php
2 class Example
3 {
4 protected $db;
5
6 public function __construct()
7 {
8 global $db;
9 $this->db = $db;
10 }
11
12 public function fetch()
13 {
14 return $this->db->query(...);
15 }
16 }
17 ?>
```

> If there are multiple `global` calls inside the same class, we should convert all of them to properties in that class. We want to work *one class at a time* as this makes later parts of this process easier.

Spot check the class

Now that we have converted `global` calls to properties in this one class, we need to test the application to make sure it still works. However, since there is no formal testing system in place yet, we pseudo-test or spot check by browsing to or otherwise invoking files that use the modified class.

If we like, we can make an interim commit here once we are sure the application still works. We will not push to the central repository or notify QA just yet; all we want is a point to which we can roll back if later changes need to be undone.

Convert global properties to constructor parameters

Once we ascertain that the class works with the properties in place, we need to convert the `global` calls in the constructor to use passed parameters instead. Given our `Example` class above, the converted version might look like this:

classes/Example.php
```
1 <?php
2 class Example
3 {
4 protected $db;
5
6 public function __construct(Db $db)
7 {
8 $this->db = $db;
9 }
10
11 public function fetch()
12 {
13 return $this->db->query(...);
14 }
15 }
16 ?>
```

All we have done here is remove the `global` call, and added a constructor parameter. We need to do this for every `global` in the constructor.

Since the `global` is for a particular class of object, we typehint the parameter to that class (in this case `Db`). If possible, we should typehint to an interface instead, so if the `Db` object implements a *DbInterface*, we should typehint to *DbInterface*. This will help with testing and later refactoring. We may also typehint to `array` or `callable` as appropriate. Not all `global` calls are for typed values, so not all parameters will need typehints (e.g., when the parameter is expected to be a string).

Convert instantiations to use parameters

After converting `global` variables to constructor parameters, we will find that every instantiation of the class throughout the legacy application is now broken. This is because the constructor signature has changed. With that in mind, we now need to search *the entire codebase* (not just the classes) for instantiations of the class, and change the instantiations to the new signature.

To search for instantiations, we use our project-wide search facility to find uses of the `new` keyword with our class name using a regular expression:

```
new\s+Example\W
```

The expression searches for the `new` keyword, followed by at least one character of whitespace, followed by a terminating non-word character (such as a parenthesis, space, or semicolon).

Formatting Issues

Legacy codebases are notorious for having messed-up formatting, which means this expression is imperfect in some situations. The expression as given here may not find instantiations where, for example, the `new` keyword is on one line, and the class name is the very next thing but is on the next line, not the same line.

Class Aliases With use

In PHP 5.3 and later, classes may be aliased to another class name with a use statement, like so:

```php
1 <?php
2 use Example as Foobar;
3 // ...
4 $foo = new Foobar;
5 ?>
```

In this case, we need to do two searches: one for use \s+Example\ s+as to discover the various aliases, and a second search for the new keyword with the alias.

As we discover instantiations of the class in the codebase, we modify them to pass the parameters as needed. If, for example, a page script looks like this:

page_script.php
```php
1 <?php
2 // a setup file that creates a $db variable
3 require 'includes/setup.php';
4 // ...
5 $example = new Example;
6 ?>
```

We need to add the parameter to the instantiation:

page_script.php
```php
1 <?php
2 // a setup file that creates a $db variable
3 require 'includes/setup.php';
4 // ...
5 $example = new Example($db);
6 ?>
```

The new instantiations need to match the new constructor signature, so if the constructor takes more than one parameter, we need to pass all of the parameters.

Spot check, Commit, Push, Notify QA

We have reached the end of the conversion process for this class. We need to spot check the converted instantiations now, but (as always) this is not an automated process, so we need to run or otherwise invoke the files with the changed code. If there are problems, go back and fix them.

Once we have done so, and are sure there are no errors, we can commit the changed code, push it to our central repository, and notify QA that it needs to run its test suite over the legacy application.

Do ... While

That is the process to convert a single class from using global calls to using dependency injection. Go back through the class files and find the next class with a global call and begin the process again. Continue to do so until there are no more global calls in the classes.

Common Questions

What if we find a global in a static method?

Sometimes we will find that a static class method uses a global variable like so:

```
1 <?php
2 class Foo
3 {
4 static public function doSomething($baz)
5 {
6 global $bar;
7 // ... do something with $bar ...
8 }
9 }
10 ?>
```

This is a problem because there is no constructor to which we can move the global variable as a property. There are two options here.

The first option is to pass all the needed globals as parameters on the static method itself, thereby changing the signature of the method:

```
1 <?php
2 class Foo
```

```
3 {
4 static public function doSomething($bar, $baz)
5 {
6 // ... do something with $bar ...
7 }
8 }
9 ?>
```

We would then search the codebase for all uses of `Foo::doSomething(` and pass the `$bar` value each time. For that reason, I suggest adding the new parameters to the *beginning* of the signature, rather than to the end, because it makes search-and-replace much easier. For example:

Search for:

```
Foo::doSomething\(
```

Replace with:

```
Foo::doSomething\($bar,
```

The second option is to change the class so that it must be instantiated, and make all the methods instance methods. The class, after conversion, might look like this:

```
1 <?php
2 class Foo
3 {
4 protected $bar;
5
6 public function __construct($bar)
7 {
8 $this->bar = $bar;
9 }
10
11 public function doSomething($baz)
12 {
13 // ... do something with $this->bar ...
14 }
15 }
16 ?>
```

After that, we would need to:

1. Search the codebase for all `Foo::` static calls;

2. Create instances of Foo with its `$bar` dependency (e.g., `$foo = new Foo($bar);`) before those static calls are made, and

3. Replace calls of `Foo::doSomething()` with `$foo->doSomething()`.

Is there an alternative conversion process?

The process described above is a class-by-class process, where we first move the globals in a single class to the constructor, then change from global properties to instance properties in that class, and finally change instantiations of that class.

Alternatively, we might choose a modified process:

1. Change all global variables to properties in all classes, then test/commit/ push/QA.

2. Change all global properties to constructor parameters *in all classes*, and change instantiations *of all classes*, then test/commit/push/QA.

This may be a reasonable alternative for smaller codebases, but it comes with some problems, such as:

1. The search for `global` calls becomes a little more difficult while converting globals to properties, because we will see the `global` keyword in both the converted and unconverted classes.

2. The commits for each major step will be much larger and harder to read.

For these reasons and others, I think it's better to stay with the process as described. It works with large and small codebases, and keeps incremental changes in smaller easier-to-read portions.

What about class names in variables?

Sometimes we will find that classes are instantiated based on variable values. For example, this creates an object based on the value of the `$class` variable:

page_script.php
```
1 <?php
2 // $type is defined earlier in the file, and then:
3 $class = $type . '_Record';
4 $record = new $class;
5 ?>
```

If $type is Blog, then the $record object will be of the class Blog_Record.

This kind of thing is very difficult to discover when searching for class instantiations to convert to using constructor parameters. I'm afraid I have no good advice for automatically finding these kinds of instantiations. The best we can do is to search for new\s+\$ without any class name, and modify the calls individually by hand.

What about superglobals?

Superglobals represent a challenging special case when removing global variables. They are automatically global within every scope, so they carry all the drawbacks of globals. We won't find them with a search for the global keyword (although we can search for them by name). Because they truly are global, we need to remove them from our classes just as much as we need to remove the global keyword.

We could pass a copy of each superglobal into the class when we need it. In cases where we need only one this might be fine, but frequently we need two or three or more superglobals. In addition, passing a copy of $_SESSION will not work as expected; PHP uses the actual superglobal of $_SESSION for writing session data, so changes to the copy will not be honored.

As a solution, we can use a Request data structure class. The Request encapsulates a copy of each of the non-$_SESSION superglobals. At the same time, the Request maintains a reference to $_SESSION so that changes to the object property are honored by the real $_SESSION superglobal.

> Note that the Request is not an HTTP request object per se. It is merely a representation of the request environment for PHP, including server, environment, and session values, many of which are not found in HTTP messages.

For example, say we have a class that uses $_POST, $_SERVER, and $_SESSION:

```php
1 <?php
2 class PostTracker
3 {
4 public function incrementPostCount()
5 {
6 if ($_SERVER['REQUEST_METHOD'] != 'POST') {
7 return;
8 }
9
10 if (isset($_POST['increment_count'])) {
```

```
11 $_SESSION['post_count'] ++;
12 }
13 }
14 }
15 ?>
```

To replace these calls, we first create a shared `Request` object in our setup code.

includes/setup.php
```
1 <?php
2 // ...
3 $request = new \Mlaphp\Request($GLOBALS);
4 // ...
5 ?>
```

We can then decouple from the superglobals by injecting that shared `Request` object in to any class that needs it, and use the `Request` properties instead of the superglobals:

```
1 <?php
2 use Mlaphp\Request;
3
4 class PostTracker
5 {
6 public function __construct(Request $request)
7 {
8 $this->request = $request;
9 }
10
11 public function incrementPostCount()
12 {
13 if ($this->request->server['REQUEST_METHOD'] != 'POST') {
14 return;
15 }
16
17 if (isset($this->request->post['increment_count'])) {
18 $this->request->session['post_count'] ++;
19 }
20 }
21 }
22 ?>
```

> If it is important to maintain changes to the superglobal values across scopes, be sure to use the same `Request` object throughout the application. Modifications to the values in one `Request` object will not be reflected in a different `Request` object, except for `$session` values (because they are all references to `$_SESSION`).

What about $GLOBALS?

There is one more superglobal that PHP provides: `$GLOBALS`. Using this superglobal inside our classes and methods should be treated as a use of the `global` keyword. For example, `$GLOBALS['foo']` is the equivalent of `global $foo`. We should remove it from our classes in just the same way as we do with uses of `global`.

Review and next steps

At this point, we have removed all `global` calls in our classes, as well as all uses of superglobals. This is another big improvement in the quality of our codebase. We know that variables can be modified locally and not affect other parts of the codebase.

However, our classes may still have hidden dependencies in them. In order to make our classes more testable, we need to discover and reveal those dependencies. That is the subject of the next chapter.

6

Replace new with Dependency Injection

Even though we have removed all global calls in our classes, they are likely to retain other hidden dependencies. In particular, we are probably creating new object instances in inappropriate locations, tightly coupling the classes together. These things make it much harder to write tests and to see what the internal dependencies are.

Embedded instantiation

After converting the global calls in a hypothetical *ItemsGateway* class, we might have something like this:

classes/ItemsGateway.php
```php
1 <?php
2 class ItemsGateway
3 {
4 protected $db_host;
5 protected $db_user;
6 protected $db_pass;
7 protected $db;
8
9 public function __construct($db_host, $db_user, $db_pass)
10 {
11 $this->db_host = $db_host;
12 $this->db_user = $db_user;
13 $this->db_pass = $db_pass;
14 $this->db = new Db($this->db_host, $this->db_user, $this->db_pass);
15 }
16
```

```
17 public function selectAll()
18 {
19 $rows = $this->db->query("SELECT * FROM items ORDER BY id");
20 $item_collection = array();
21 foreach ($rows as $row) {
22 $item_collection[] = new Item($row);
23 }
24 return $item_collection;
25 }
26 }
27 ?>
```

There are two dependency injection issues here:

1. First, the class probably got converted from a function that used global $db_host, $db_user, $db_pass and then constructed a Db object internally. Our initial pass at removing global calls got rid of the globals, but it left this Db dependency in place. This is what we will call a one-time creation dependency.

2. Second, the selectAll() method creates new Item objects, and as such is dependent on the Item class. We cannot see this dependency from the outside of the class. This is what we will call a repeated creation dependency.

> As far as I know, the terms one-time creation dependency and repeated creation dependency are not industry-standard terms. They are for the purposes of this book only. Please inform the author if you are aware of similar concepts that have industry-standard terms.

The point of dependency injection is to push the dependencies in from the outside, thereby revealing the dependencies in our classes. Using a new keyword inside a class is in opposition to that idea, so we need to work through the codebase to remove that keyword from our non-Factory classes.

> **What is a Factory Object?**
>
> One of the keys to dependency injection is that an object may either create other objects, *or* it may operate on other objects, *but not both*. Any time we need to create an object inside another object, we let that work be done by something called a *Factory* with a newInstance() method and inject that *Factory* into the object that needs to do creation. The new keyword is restricted to being used inside *Factory* objects. This allows us to switch out *Factory* objects any time we need to create different kinds of objects.

The replacement process

The next step, then, is to remove all use of `new` keyword from our non-*Factory* classes, and inject the necessary dependencies instead. We will also use *Factory* objects as needed to deal with repeated creation dependencies. This is the general process we will follow:

1. Find a class with the `new` keyword in it. If the class is already a `Factory`, we can ignore it and move on.

2. For each one-time creation in the class:

    ° Extract each instantiation to a constructor parameter.

    ° Assign the constructor parameter to a property.

    ° Remove any constructor parameters and class properties that are used only for the `new` call.

3. For each repeated creation in the class:

    ° Extract each block of creation code to a new `Factory` class.

    ° Create a constructor parameter for each `Factory` and assign it to a property.

    ° Modify the previous creation logic in the class to use the *Factory*.

4. Change all instantiation calls for the modified class throughout the project so that the necessary dependency objects are passed to the constructor.

5. Spot check, commit, push, and notify QA.

6. Repeat with the next `new` call that is not inside a *Factory* object.

Find a new keyword

As in other steps, we begin this one by using our project-wide search facility to look for the `new` keyword in our class files using the following regular expression:

Search for:

```
new\s+
```

We have two kinds of creation to look for: one-time and repeated. How can we tell the difference? In general:

- If the instantiation is assigned to a property, and is never changed, it is most likely a one-time creation. Generally, we see this in constructors.

- If the instantiation occurs in a non-constructor method, it is most likely a repeated creation, because it occurs each time the method is called.

Extract One-Time creation to dependency injection

Let's say we find the *ItemsGateway* class listed above when we search for the new keyword, and encounter the constructor:

```
classes/ItemsGateway.php
1  <?php
2  class ItemsGateway
3  {
4  protected $db_host;
5  protected $db_user;
6  protected $db_pass;
7  protected $db;
8
9  public function __construct($db_host, $db_user, $db_pass)
10 {
11 $this->db_host = $db_host;
12 $this->db_user = $db_user;
13 $this->db_pass = $db_pass;
14 $this->db = new Db($this->db_host, $this->db_user, $this->db_pass);
15 }
16 // ...
17 }
18 ?>
```

On examining the class, we find that $this->db is assigned once as a property. This appears to be a one-time creation. In addition, it appears that at least some of the existing constructor parameters are used only for the Db instantiation.

We proceed to remove the instantiation call entirely, along with the properties used only for the instantiation call, and replace the constructor parameters with a single Db parameter:

```
classes/ItemsGateway.php
1  <?php
2  class ItemsGateway
3  {
4  protected $db;
5
6  public function __construct(Db $db)
7  {
8  $this->db = $db;
9  }
10
```

```
11 // ...
12 }
13 ?>
```

Extract repeated creation to factory

If we find a repeated creation instead of a one-time creation, we have a different task to accomplish. Let's return to the *ItemsGateway* class, but this time we'll look at the `selectAll()` method.

classes/ItemsGateway.php
```
1 <?php
2 class ItemsGateway
3 {
4 protected $db;
5
6 public function __construct(Db $db)
7 {
8 $this->db = $db;
9 }
10
11 public function selectAll()
12 {
13 $rows = $this->db->query("SELECT * FROM items ORDER BY id");
14 $item_collection = array();
15 foreach ($rows as $row) {
16 $item_collection[] = new Item($row);
17 }
18 return $item_collection;
19 }
20 }
21 ?>
```

We can see here that the `new` keyword occurs in a loop inside a method. This is clearly a case of repeated creation.

First, we extract the creation code to its own new class. Because the code creates an `Item` object, we will call the class *ItemFactory*. In it, we will create a method for returning new instances of `Item` objects:

```
classes/ItemFactory.php
1 <?php
2 class ItemFactory
3 {
4 public function newInstance(array $item_data)
```

```
5 {
6 return new Item($item_data);
7 }
8 }
9 ?>
```

> The only purpose of a *Factory* is to create new objects. It should not have any other functionality. It will be tempting to place other behavior in a `Factory` in a bid to centralize common logic. Resist this temptation!

Now that we have extracted the creation code to a separate class, we will modify the *ItemsGateway* to take an *ItemFactory* parameter, retain it in a property, and use the *ItemFactory* to create *Item* objects.

classes/ItemsGateway.php

```php
1 <?php
2 class ItemsGateway
3 {
4 protected $db;
5
6 protected $item_factory;
7
8 public function __construct(Db $db, ItemFactory $item_factory)
9 {
10 $this->db = $db;
11 $this->item_factory = $item_factory;
12 }
13
14 public function selectAll()
15 {
16 $rows = $this->db->query("SELECT * FROM items ORDER BY id");
17 $item_collection = array();
18 foreach ($rows as $row) {
19 $item_collection[] = $this->item_factory->newInstance($row);
20 }
21 return $item_collection;
22 }
23 }
24 ?>
```

Change instantiation calls

Because we have changed the constructor signature, all the existing instantiations of *ItemsGateway* are now broken. We need to find all the places in the code where the *ItemsGateway* class is instantiated, and change the instantiations to pass a properly-constructed Db object and an *ItemFactory*.

To do so, we use our project-wide search facility to search using a regular expression for our changed class name:

Search for:

```
new\s+ItemsGateway\(
```

Doing so will give us a list of all instantiations in the project. We need to review each result and change it by hand to instantiate the dependencies and pass them to the *ItemsGateway*.

For example, if a page script from the search results looks like this:

page_script.php
```
1 <?php
2 // $db_host, $db_user, and $db_pass are defined in the setup file
3 require 'includes/setup.php';
4
5 // ...
6
7 // create a gateway
8 $items_gateway = new ItemsGateway($db_host, $db_user, $db_pass);
9
10 // ...
11 ?>
```

We need to change it to something more like this:

page_script.php
```
1 <?php
2 // $db_host, $db_user, and $db_pass are defined in the setup file
3 require 'includes/setup.php';
4
5 // ...
6
7 // create a gateway with its dependencies
8 $db = new Db($db_host, $db_user, $db_pass);
9 $item_factory = new ItemFactory;
10 $items_gateway = new ItemsGateway($db, $item_factory);
```

```
11
12 // ...
13 ?>
```

Do this for each instantiation of the changed class.

Spot Check, Commit, Push, Notify QA

Now that we have changed the class and the instantiations of the class throughout the codebase, we need to make sure our legacy application works. Again, we have no formal testing process in place, so we need to run or otherwise invoke the parts of the application that use the changed class and look for errors.

Once we feel sure that the application still operates properly, we commit the code, push it to our central repository, and notify QA that we are ready for them to test our new additions.

Do ... While

Search for the next new keyword in a class, and start the process all over again. When we find that new keywords exist only in *Factory* classes, our job is complete.

Common Questions

What About Exceptions and SPL Classes?

In this chapter, we concentrate on removing all use of the new keyword, except inside *Factory* objects. I believe there are two reasonable exceptions to this rule: *Exception* classes themselves, and certain built-in PHP classes, such as the SPL classes.

It would be perfectly consistent with the process described in this chapter to create an ExceptionFactory class, inject it into objects that throw exceptions, and then use the ExceptionFactory to create the Exception objects to be thrown. This strikes even me as going a bit too far. I think that Exception objects are a reasonable exception to the rule of no new outside Factory objects.

Similarly, I think built-in PHP classes are also frequently an exception to the rule. While it would be nice to have, say, an *ArrayObjectFactory* or an *ArrayIteratorFactory* to create *ArrayObject* and *ArrayIterator* classes that are provided by SPL itself, it may be a little too much. Creating these kinds of objects directly inside the objects that use them is usually all right.

However, we need to be careful. Creating a complex or otherwise powerful object like a PDO connection directly inside the class that needs it is probably overstepping our bounds. It's tough to describe a good rule of thumb here; when in doubt, err on the side of dependency injection.

What about Intermediary Dependencies?

Sometime we will discover classes that have dependencies, and the dependencies themselves have dependencies. These intermediary dependencies are passed to the outside class, which carries them along only so that the internal objects can be instantiated with them.

For example, say we have a Service class that needs an *ItemsGateway*, which itself needs a Db connection. Before removing global variables, the Service class might have looked like this:

classes/Service.php
```php
1 <?php
2 class Service
3 {
4 public function doThis()
5 {
6 // ...
7 $db = global $db;
8 $items_gateway = new ItemsGateway($db);
9 $items = $items_gateway->selectAll();
10 // ...
11 }
12
13 public function doThat()
14 {
15 // ...
16 $db = global $db;
17 $items_gateway = new ItemsGateway($db);
18 $items = $items_gateway->selectAll();
19 // ...
20 }
21 }
22 ?>
```

After removing `global` variables, we are left with a `new` keyword, but we still need the `Db` object as a dependency for *ItemsGateway*:

classes/Service.php
```php
1  <?php
2  class Service
3  {
4  protected $db;
5
6  public function __construct(Db $db)
7  {
8  $this->db = $db;
9  }
10
11  public function doThis()
12  {
13  // ...
14  $items_gateway = new ItemsGateway($this->db);
15  $items = $items_gateway->selectAll();
16  // ...
17  }
18
19  public function doThat()
20  {
21  // ...
22  $items_gateway = new ItemsGateway($this->db);
23  $items = $items_gateway->selectAll();
24  // ...
25  }
26  }
27  ?>
```

How do we successfully remove the `new` keyword here? The *ItemsGateway* needs a `Db` connection. The `Db` connection is never used by the `Service` directly; it is used only for building the *ItemsGateway*.

The solution in cases like this is to inject a fully-constructed *ItemsGateway*. First, we modify the `Service` class to receive its real dependency, the *ItemsGateway*:

classes/Service.php
```php
1  <?php
2  class Service
3  {
4  protected $items_gateway;
5
```

```
6 public function __construct(ItemsGateway $items_gateway)
7 {
8 $this->items_gateway = $items_gateway;
9 }
10
11 public function doThis()
12 {
13 // ...
14 $items = $this->items_gateway->selectAll();
15 // ...
16 }
17
18 public function doThat()
19 {
20 // ...
21 $items = $this->items_gateway->selectAll();
22 // ...
23 }
24 }
25 ?>
```

Second, throughout the entire legacy application, we change all instantiations of the *Service* to pass an *ItemsGateway*.

For example, a page script might have done this when using `global` variables everywhere:

page_script.php (globals)
```
1 <?php
2 // defines the $db connection
3 require 'includes/setup.php';
4
5 // creates the service with globals
6 $service = new Service;
7 ?>
```

And then we changed it to inject the intermediary dependency after removing globals:

page_script.php (intermediary dependency)
```
1 <?php
2 // defines the $db connection
3 require 'includes/setup.php';
4
5 // inject the Db object for the internal ItemsGateway creation
6 $service = new Service($db);
7 ?>
```

But we should finally change it to inject the real dependency:

page_script.php (real dependency)

```php
1 <?php
2 // defines the $db connection
3 require 'includes/setup.php';
4
5 // create the gateway dependency and then the service
6 $items_gateway = new ItemsGateway($db);
7 $service = new Service($items_gateway);
8 ?>
```

Isn't this a lot of code?

I sometimes hear the complaint that using dependency injection means a lot of extra code to do the same thing as before.

It's true. Having a call like this, where the class manages its own dependencies internally.

Without dependency injection:

```php
1 <?php
2 $items_gateway = new ItemsGateway;
3 ?>
```

This is obviously less code than using dependency injection by creating the dependencies and using `Factory` objects.

With dependency injection:

```php
1 <?php
2 $db = new Db($db_host, $db_user, $db_pass);
3 $item_factory = new ItemFactory;
4 $items_gateway = new ItemsGateway($db, $item_factory);
5 ?>
```

The real issue here, though, is not more code. The issues are more testable,more clear, and more decoupled.

In looking at the first example, how can we tell what *ItemsGateway* needs to operate? What other parts of the system will it affect? It's very difficult to tell without examining the entire class and looking for `global` and `new` keywords.

In looking at the second example, it is very easy to tell what the class needs to operate, what we can expect it to create, and what parts of the system it interacts with. These things additionally make it easier to test the class later.

Should a factory create collections?

In the examples above, our `Factory` class only creates a single `newInstance()` of
an object. If we regularly create collections of objects, it may be reasonable to add
a `newCollection()` method to our `Factory`. For example, given our *ItemFactory*
above, we may do something like the following:

classes/ItemFactory.php

```php
1  <?php
2  class ItemFactory
3  {
4  public function newInstance(array $item_data)
5  {
6  return new Item($item_data);
7  }
8
9  public function newCollection(array $items_data)
10 {
11 $collection = array();
12 foreach ($items_data as $item_data) {
13 $collection[] = $this->newInstance($item_data);
14 }
15 return $collection;
16 }
17 }
18 ?>
```

We may go so far as to create an `ItemCollection` class for the collection instead
of using an array. If so, it would be reasonable to use a `new` keyword inside our
`ItemFactory` to create the `ItemCollection` instance. (The `ItemCollection` class is
omitted here).

classes/ItemFactory.php

```php
1  <?php
2  class ItemFactory
3  {
4  public function newInstance(array $item_data)
5  {
6  return new Item($item_data);
7  }
8
9  public function newCollection(array $item_rows)
10 {
11 $collection = new ItemCollection;
12 foreach ($item_rows as $item_data) {
```

```
13 $item = $this->newInstance($item_data);
14 $collection->append($item);
15 }
16 return $collection;
17 }
18 }
19 ?>
```

Indeed, we may wish to have a separate *ItemCollectionFactory*, using an injected *ItemFactory* to create Item objects, with its own newInstance() method to return a new *ItemCollection*.

There are many variations on the proper use of Factory objects. The key is to keep object creation (and related operations) separate from object manipulation.

Can we automate all these Injections?

All the dependency injection we have been doing so far has been manual injection, where we create the dependencies ourselves and then inject them as we create the objects we need. This can be a tedious process. Who wants to create a Db object over and over again just so it can be injected into a variety of Gateway classes? Isn't there some way to automate that?

Yes, there is. It is called a Container. A Container may go by various synonyms indicating how it is to be used. A Dependency Injection Container is intended to be used always-and-only outside the non-Factory classes, whereas an identical Container implementation going by the name Service Locator is intended to be used inside non-Factory objects.

Using a Container brings distinct advantages:

- We can create shared services that are instantiated only when they are called. For example, the Container can house a Db instance that only gets created when we ask the Container for a database connection; the connection is created once and then reused over and over again.

- We can put complex object creation inside the Container, where objects that need multiple services for their constructor parameters can retrieve those services from the Container inside their own creation logic.

But using a `Container` has disadvantages as well:

- We have to drastically change how we think about our object creation, and where those objects live in the application. In the end this is a good thing, but it can be trouble in the interim.

- A `Container` used as a Service Locator replaces our `global` variables with a fancy new toy that has many of the same problems as `global`. The `Container` hides dependencies because it is called only from inside the class that needs dependencies.

At this stage of modernizing our legacy application it can be very tempting to start using a `Container` to automate dependency injection for use. I sugest that we do not add one just now, because so much of our legacy application remains to be modernized. We will add one eventually, but it will be as the very last step of our modernization process.

Review and next steps

We have now made great strides in modernizing our application. Removing `global` and `new` keywords in favor of dependency injections has already improved the quality of the codebase and made tracking down bugs a lot easier, if only because modifying a variable over here no longer causes a variable over there to be affected at a distance. Our page scripts might be somewhat longer, because we have to create the dependencies, but we can now see exactly what parts of the system we are interacting with much more clearly.

Our next step is to examine our newly refactored classes and start writing tests for them. That way, when we start making changes to the classes, we will know if we broke any previously existing behavior.

7
Write Tests

At this point, our legacy application has been partially modernized so that we have all existing classes in a central location. Those classes now enjoy freedom from `global` and `new` using dependency injection. The proper thing to do now is to write tests for these classes so that, if we ever need to change them, we know that their pre-existing behavior remains intact.

Fighting test resistance

We are probably not eager to spend time writing tests right now. We don't want to lose the forward momentum we are feeling. Just as we believe we are making some real progress, stopping to write tests feels like make-work. It takes away from the joy of making yet another series of improvements to the awful codebase that we have been suffering under for so long.

The resistance to writing tests is understandable. I myself was only a slow convert to automated testing. If one is not used to it, the act of writing tests feels alien, unfamiliar, challenging, and unproductive. It is very easy to say, I can see the code is working, because the application is working.

And yet if we do not write tests, we are condemning ourselves to continued rounds of suffering later. We are enabling a particular kind of awfulness in our legacy application: that feeling of dread we feel when we change one part of the application, not knowing what other parts of the application are going to break as a result.

So while it may be true that writing tests sucks, it is also true that "having written tests" is awesome. It is awesome because, as we make changes to our classes, we can run an automated test suite, and it will tell us immediately if anything has broken after a change.

The way of Testivus

Even if we are already familiar with writing tests, all of the dogma that surrounds testing can be intimidating:

- Do not interact with the file system; build a virtual file system instead.
- Do not interact with the database; build a set of data fixtures instead.
- Rewrite your classes to use interfaces instead of concrete classes, and write test doubles for all the dependencies.

These are the kinds of dogmatic commands that make testing seem like an insurmountable challenge. Surely we can build our tests later when everything else is done! The problem is that there will never be a point when everything else is done, and so the tests will never come into being.

As an antidote to the dogma of testing commandments, I suggest following *The Way Of Testivus* (`http://www.artima.com/weblogs/viewpost.jsp?thread=203994`) instead. The core message of *The Way of Testivus* is More testing karma, less testing dogma.

These are the major points we need to take from *Testivus* in regard to modernizing our legacy application:

- The best time to test is when the code is fresh.
- Write the test that needs to be written.
- An imperfect test today is better than a perfect test someday.
- Write the test you can today.

The code in the classes is stale. That code is part of a legacy application, after all. But now that we have spent so much time reorganizing the classes and removing their `global` and `new` keywords in favor of dependency injection, the code in those classes has been made fresh again in our minds. Now is the time to write the tests for these classes, while their operation is still in recent memory.

We should not get hung up on writing proper unit tests that adhere to every commandment of testing dogma. Instead, we should write the best test we can, even if the test is imperfect:

- If we can write a characterization test that only checks the output as-it-is, then we should do so.
- If we can write a functional or integration test that interacts with the database, network, or file system, then we should do so.

- If we can write a loose unit test that combines concrete classes, then we should do so.

- If we can write a strict unit test that uses test doubles to fully isolate the tested class, then we should do so.

An imperfect test can be perfected as we become more adept at testing. A test that does not exist cannot be perfected at all.

We will write the tests we can, while we can, as soon as we can. Waiting to write tests will only increase the inertia against writing tests. The code will grow more stale in our mind, making the tests harder to write. Writing tests today will give us a sense of accomplishment and increase our inertia in favor of writing tests.

Setting up a test suite

It is not within the scope of this book to fully explain the technique and methodology of writing tests. Instead, we will review a very brief summary of the process involved in setting up the automated test suite and writing a simple test. For a more thorough treatment of testing in PHP, refer to *The Grumpy Programmer's PHPUnit Cookbook* (`http://grumpy-phpunit.com/`)by *Chris Hartjes*.

Install PHPUnit

There are many different testing systems in PHP land, but the most commonly used one is PHPUnit. We need to install PHPUnit on our development and testing servers in order to write and execute our tests. The full installation instructions are at the PHPUnit site.

One easy way to install PHPUnit is via Composer:

```
$ composer global require phpunit/phpunit=~4.5
```

Another way is to install a `.phar` of PHPUnit directly:

```
$ wget https://phar.phpunit.de/phpunit.phar
$ chmod +x phpunit.phar
$ sudo mv phpunit.phar /usr/local/bin/phpunit
```

Create a tests/ directory

Once we have PHPUnit installed, we need to create a tests/ directory in our legacy application. The name and location do not matter so much as the fact that the purpose and place are obvious. The most obvious place is probably at the root of the legacy application, though it should not be directly accessible by browsers.

Within the tests/ directory, we need to create a subdirectory named for our central class directory location. If all our application classes are in a directory named classes/, then we should have a tests/classes/ directory. The idea is for our testing structure to mimic the structure of our application classes.

In addition to the tests/classes/ subdirectory, the tests/ directory should contain two files. The first is a bootstrap.php file that PHPUnit will execute when it runs. Its purpose is to help set up the execution environment for the tests. By default, PHPUnit will not use the application autoloader code, so creating and registering the autoloader is a classic use for the bootstrap.php file. Here is an example using the autoloader from an earlier chapter:

tests/bootstrap.php

```
1 <?php
2 require "../classes/Mlaphp/Autoloader.php";
3 $loader = new \Mlaphp\Autoloader;
4 spl_autoload_register(array($loader, 'load'));
5 ?>
```

Also in the tests/ directory, we need to create a phpunit.xml file. This tells PHPUnit how to bootstrap itself and where the tests are located:

tests/phpunit.xml

```
1 <phpunit bootstrap="./bootstrap.php">
2 <testsuites>
3 <testsuite>
4 <directory>./classes</directory>
5 </testsuite>
6 </testsuites>
7 </phpunit>
```

After creating the tests/ directory and its contents, our legacy application directory structure should look something like this:

/path/to/app/

```
classes/          # our central class directory location
Auth.php          # class Auth { ... }
Db.php            # class Db { ... }
```

```
Mlaphp/
Autoloader.php    # A hypothetical autoloader class
Role.php          # class Role { ... }
User.php          # class User { ... }
foo/
bar/
baz.php           # a page script
includes/         # a common "includes" directory
setup.php         # setup code
index.php         # a page script
tests/            # tests directory
bootstrap.php     # phpunit bootstrap code
classes/          # test cases
phpunit.xml       # phpunit setup file
```

Pick a class to test

Now that we have a `tests/` directory in place, we can actually write a test for one of our application classes. The easiest way to get started is to pick a class that has no dependencies. We should be familiar enough with the codebase at this point that we know which classes have dependencies and which do not. If we cannot find a class that has no dependencies, we should pick the one with the fewest dependencies, or with the least-complex dependencies.

What we want to do here is *start small* and get some early wins. Each win will give us the drive and motivation to continue with larger, more complex tests. These smaller wins will accumulate into a final big win: a fully-tested set of classes.

Write a test case

Let's say we have picked a class named `Foo` that has no dependencies, and that it has a method called `doSomething()`. We are now going to write a test for this class method.

First, we create a skeleton test file in our `tests/classes/` directory. Its location should mimic the location of the class being tested. We add `Test` to the end of the class name, and extend `PHPUnitFramework_TestCase_` so that we have access to the various `assert*()` methods in the testing class:

tests/classes/FooTest.php
```
1 <?php
2 class FooTest extends \PHPUnit_Framework_TestCase
3 {
4 }
5 ?>
```

If we try to run our tests now with phpunit, the test will fail because it has no test methods in it:

```
tests $ phpunit
PHPUnit 3.7.30 by Sebastian Bergmann.
Configuration read from tests/phpunit.xml
F
Time: 45 ms, Memory: 2.75Mb
There was 1 failure:
1) Warning
No tests found in class "FooTest".
FAILURES!
Tests: 1, Assertions: 0, Failures: 1.
tests $
```

Believe it or not, this is just fine! As *The Way Of Testivus* tells us, we rejoice when our tests pass, and we rejoice when they fail. The failure here tells us that PHPUnit has successfully found our test class, but did not find any tests in that class. That tells us what to do next.

The next step is to add a test method for a public method of the class being tested. All test methods begin with the word test, so we will test the doSomething() method using a method named testDoSomething(). In it, we will create an instance of the _Foo_ class, invoke its public doSomething() method, and assert that its actual output is the same as what we expect it to be:

tests/classes/FooTest.php
```
1 <?php
2 class FooTest extends \PHPUnit_Framework_TestCase
3 {
4 public function testDoSomething()
5 {
6 $foo = new Foo;
7 $expect = 'Did the thing!';
8 $actual = $foo->doSomething();
9 $this->assertSame($expect, $actual);
10 }
11 }
12 ?>
```

Now we can run our test suite again with phpunit. As long as the doSomething() method returns the string Did the thing! then our test will pass.

```
tests $ phpunit
PHPUnit 3.7.30 by Sebastian Bergmann.
Configuration read from tests/phpunit.xml

.

Time: 30 ms, Memory: 2.75Mb
OK (1 test, 1 assertion)
tests $
```

We rejoice because our tests have passed!

If doSomething() ever returns anything different, then the test will fail. This means that if we change doSomething() in the course of our following work, we will know that its behavior has changed. We will rejoice in its failure, knowing that we have caught a bug before it went into production, and then fix the code until all the tests pass.

Do ... While

After we write a passing test, we commit it to revision control and push it to our central repository. We continue writing tests for each public method in the application class, committing and pushing as we go. When all the public methods in the application class have passing tests, we pick another class to test, and begin again with a new test class.

Common Questions

Can we skip this step and do it later?

No.

Come On, Really, Can We Do This Later?

Look, I get it. I really do. Testing feels unrewarding at this point in our modernization process. If the entire rest of the chapter has not convinced you of the benefit of tests, then there's not much else I can say to convince you now. If you want to skip this step, you're going to skip it no matter what advice you read here.

So let us assume that our reasons for avoiding tests at this point are perfectly sensible and well-adjusted to our particular context. With that in mind, let's take a look at some things we can do to get those tests done, if not now then over the course of the project. Go on to the next chapter (unadvisedly!) but then commit to one or more of the following options:

1. Complete at least one new test class per day.

2. Each time we use a method in the codebase, check to see if there is a test for it. If there is not, write one before using the method.

3. As we fix a bug or build a feature, create a list of methods used over the course of the task, then write tests for those methods when the task is complete.

4. When we add a new class method, write a corresponding test for it.

5. Delegate the writing of tests to another developer, perhaps a junior developer. Then we can have the "fun" of modernizing, and the junior developer can have the perceived boring work of writing tests, but beware ... pretty soon, the junior developer will know more about the codebase than we do.

These options allow us to build up a test suite and still feel like we are making progress elsewhere. Creating an automated test suite is a non-negotiable aspect of modernizing our legacy application. Write tests now, or write them as we go, but write them, sooner rather than later.

What about hard-to-test classes?

Even with dependency injection in place, some of the classes in the legacy application are going to be hard to write tests for. There are lots of ways in which the classes can be hard to test and I cannot do the solutions justice in this book. Instead, please refer to these works:

*   *Working Effectively With Legacy Code* by *Michael Feathers*. The examples throughout are in Java, but the situations are similar to those in PHP. Feathers shows how to break dependencies, introduce seams, and otherwise improve the testability of legacy classes.

*   Refactoring by Fowler et al. This one also uses Java in the examples, but thanks to Adam Culp, we have the same examples converted to PHP. As with Fowler's Patterns of Enterprise Application Architecture, the Refactoring book will give you a vocabulary to describe things you probably already know how to do, as well as introduce you to new techniques.

The information in these publications will help us improve the quality of our classes without changing the behavior of the classes.

What about our earlier characterization tests?

The tests we write as a result of this chapter are probably not a replacement for any existing characterization tests from the chapter on Prerequisites. Having the two sets of tests is likely to be a blessing, not a curse. At some point, the characterization tests may end up being converted to acceptance tests for use by the QA team. Until then, run both sets of tests from time to time.

Should we test private and protected methods?

Probably not. There are dogmatic reasons for this that I will not go into here, but the short version is this: tests that inspect too deeply the internal workings of a class become difficult to work with.

Instead, we should test only the public methods on our classes. Any behavior exposed by these methods is likely to be the only behavior we care about. There are some exceptions to this rule, but at this stage in our testing career, the exceptions are less important than the rule.

Can we change a test after we write it?

The time will come when we need to change the existing behavior of an application class method. In these cases, it is all right to change the related test to suit the new behavior. However, when we do so, we must be sure to run the entire test suite, not just the tests for that application class. Running the entire test suite will help us make sure that the change does not break behavior in other classes.

Do we need to test Third-party libraries?

If our legacy application uses third-party libraries, they may already come with tests. We should run these from time to time.

If the third-party libraries do not come with tests, we may choose to write some, depending on our priorities. If we are dependent on the library behaving the same way between upgrades, it would be wise to write some tests of our own to make sure that the expected behaviors remain in place.

Building tests for a third-party library may be difficult if it is not written in an easily-testable way. If the library is free software or open source, perhaps this is an opportunity to contribute back to the project. However, our main priority is probably our own legacy application, not third-party libraries.

What about code coverage?

Code coverage is a report given by PHPUnit to tell us how many lines of code we have tested. (Strictly speaking, it tells us the number of statements that have been tested).

A particular case may only test part of a class, or part of a method, and leave some of the code untested. The parts that are tested are called the covered portions of the code and the parts that are not tested are uncovered.

It is mostly the uncovered parts of the codebase that we need to worry about. If anything in the uncovered code changes, the tests won't detect it, and so we may be open to bugs and other regressions.

If we can, we should discover the code coverage of our tests early and often. These coverage reports will help us determine what needs to be tested next, and which parts of the codebase need to be refactored so they are easier to test.

More code coverage is better. However, reaching 100% line coverage is probably not feasible (and, indeed, is not the final goal, that being 100% condition/decision coverage among other things). If we can reach 100% coverage, though, we should.

For more on this topic, please review the PHPUnit documentation on code coverage at `https://phpunit.de/manual/3.7/en/code-coverage-analysis.html`.

Review and next steps

When we have completed writing our tests, as briefly outlined in this chapter, we will have created a great trap for future bugs. Each time we run our tests, any changes to the expected behavior will stand out as failures for us to correct. This ensures that as we continue refactoring, we will be doing more good than harm to our legacy codebase as a whole.

In addition, because we now have a working test suite, we can add tests for any new behavior extracted from our legacy codebase into our application classes. Each time we create a new application class method, we will also create a passing test for that method. Each time we modify an application class method, we will run the test suite so that we can find bugs and breaks before they make it into production. We will rejoice when our tests pass, and we will rejoice when they fail; each outcome is a positive sign when it comes to modernizing our legacy application.

With that, we can continue our modernization process. The next step is to extract our data retrieval and persistence behaviors from the page scripts and into a series of classes. Generally, this means moving all our SQL calls to a separate layer.

8
Extract SQL statements to Gateways

Now that we have moved all our class-oriented functionality to a central directory location (and have a reasonable test suite for those classes) we can begin extracting more logic from our page scripts and place that logic into classes. This will have two benefits: first, we will be able to keep the various concerns of the application separated; second, we will be able to test the extracted logic so that any breaks will be easy to notice before we deploy into production.

The first of these extractions will be to move all SQL-oriented code to its own set of classes. For our purposes, SQL is a stand-in for any system of reading from and writing to a data store. This may be a no-SQL system, a CSV file, a remote resource, or anything else. We will concentrate on SQL-oriented data stores in this chapter because they are so common throughout legacy applications, but the principles apply to any form of data storage.

Embedded SQL Statements

Right now, our page scripts (and probably some of our classes) interact with a database directly with embedded SQL statements. For example, a page script might have some logic like this:

```
page_script.php
1 <?php
2 $db = new Db($db_host, $db_user, $db_pass);
3 $post_id = $_GET['post_id'];
4 $stm = "SELECT * FROM comments WHERE post_id = $post_id";
5 $rows = $db->query($stm);
```

```
6 foreach ($rows as $row) {
7 // output each row
8 }
9 ?>
```

The problems with using embedded SQL strings are numerous. Among other things, we want to:

- Test the SQL interactions in isolation from the rest of the code
- Reduce the number of repeated SQL strings throughout the codebase
- Collect related SQL commands for generalization and reuse
- Isolate and remove security flaws such as SQL injection

These problems and more lead us to the conclusion that we need to extract all our SQL-related code to an SQL layer, and replace the embedded SQL logic with calls to our SQL-related class methods. We will do this by creating a series of Gateway classes. The only thing these Gateway classes will do is get data from, and send data back to, our data sources.

The Gateway classes in this chapter are technically more like table data gateways. However, you may choose to set up any kind of Gateway that is appropriate for your data source.

The extraction process

In general, this is the process we will follow:

1. Search the entire codebase for SQL statements.
2. For each statement not already in a Gateway, move the statement and relevant logic to a related Gateway class method.
3. Write a test for the new Gateway method.
4. Replace the statement and relevant logic in the original file with a call to the Gateway class method.
5. Test, commit, push, and notify QA.
6. Repeat with the next SQL statement that is outside a Gateway class.

Search for SQL statements

As in previous chapters, we employ a project-wide search function here. Use a regular expression like the following to identify where SQL statement keywords are located in the codebase:

Search for:

`(SELECT | INSERT | UPDATE | DELETE)`

We may find that our codebase uses other SQL commands as well. If so, we should include them in the search expression.

It will be easier on us if the codebase consistently uses only one case, whether upper or lower, for SQL keywords. However, this is not always the convention in legacy code. If our codebase is inconsistent regarding the case for SQL keywords, and our project-wide search facility has a case-insensitive option, we should use that option in this search. Otherwise, we need to expand the search terms to include lower-case (and perhaps mixed-case) variations of the SQL keywords.

Finally, the search results are likely to include false positives. For example, narrative text such as "Select one of the following options" will be in the result list. We will need to examine the results individually to determine if they are SQL statements or only narrative text.

Move SQL to a Gateway class

The task of extracting the SQL to a `Gateway` is detail-oriented and context-specific. The structure of the legacy codebase itself will determine one or more correct approaches to this task.

To begin with, extracting a plain old SQL statement like the following seems straightforward:

```
1 <?php
2 $stm = "SELECT * FROM comments WHERE post_id = $post_id";
3 $rows = $db->query($stm);
4 ?>
```

But it turns out we need to make a lot of decisions even with this simple example:

- What should we name the `Gateway` class and method?
- How should we deal with parameters to the query?
- How do we avoid security flaws?
- What is the proper return value?

Namespace and Class names

To determine our namespace and class names, the first thing we need to decide is whether to organize by layer or by entity.

- If we organize by implementation layers, the top-level namespaces for our class might be `Gateway` or `DataSource\Gateway`. This naming arrangement structures the classes by their operational purpose in the codebase.

- If we organize by domain entities, the top-level namespaces would be something like `Comments`, or even `Domain\Comments`. This naming arrangement structures the classes by their purpose within the business logic domain.

The legacy codebase is likely to dictate which way to go. If there is code already organized by one or the other, then it might be better to continue in the established structure rather than redoing the existing work. We want to avoid setting up conflicting or inconsistent organizational structures in the codebase.

Of the two, I recommend organizing by domain entities. I find it more sensible to collect functionality related to specific domain entity types within their relevant namespaces, than to spread operational implementations across several namespaces. We can also further segregate the implementation pieces within the specific domain feature in a way that is not easily done when organizing by layer.

To reflect my domain entity bias, the examples in the rest of this chapter will be structured along domain lines, not implementation layers.

Once we have an organizing principle for our `Gateway` classes, we can easily find good class names. For example, our comments-related `Gateway` in PHP 5.3 and later might be named `Domain\Comments\CommentsGateway`. If we are using PHP 5.2 or earlier, we will need to avoid namespaces proper and use underscores in the class name instead; e.g., `Domain_Comments_CommentsGateway`.

Method names

Choosing an appropriate method name, however, is a little more difficult. Once again, we should look to the existing legacy codebase for a convention. The common idiom may be to `get()` the data, `find()` the data, `fetch()` the data, `select()` the data, or something else entirely.

We should stick with any existing naming convention as much as possible. While the method name itself does not matter, consistency-of-naming does. Consistency will make it easier for us to look at calls to the `Gateway` object and understand what is happening without having to read the underlying method code, and to search the codebase for data-access calls.

If our legacy codebase does not reveal a consistent pattern, it is up to us to choose a consistent naming convention for the new Gateway methods. Because the Gateway classes are supposed to be a simple layer to wrap SQL calls, the examples in this chapter will use method names like select, insert, etc. to identify the behavior being wrapped.

Finally, the method name should probably indicate the kind of select() being performed. Are we selecting one record or or all of them? Are we selecting by specific criteria? Are there other considerations on the query? These and other questions will give us hints on how to name the Gateway methods.

An initial Gateway class method

When extracting logic to a class method, we should be careful to follow all the lessons we learned about dependency injection in prior chapters. Among other things, this means: no use of globals, replacing superglobals with a Request object, no use of the new keyword outside Factory classes, and (of course) injecting objects via the constructor as needed.

Given the above naming principles, and the original SELECT statement to retrieve comment rows, we may build a Gateway that looks something like this:

classes/Domain/Comments/CommentsGateway.php

```
1 <?php
2 namespace Domain\Comments;
3
4 class CommentsGateway
5 {
6 protected $db;
7
8 public function __construct(Db $db)
9 {
10 $this->db = $db;
11 }
12
13 public function selectAllByPostId($post_id)
14 {
15 $stm = "SELECT * FROM comments WHERE post_id = {$post_id}";
16 return $this->db->query($stm);
17 }
18 }
19 ?>
```

This is practically an exact copy of the logic from the original page script. It leaves at least one major issue in place, though: it uses the input parameter directly in the query. This leaves us open to SQL injection attacks.

> **What Is SQL Injection**
>
> The classic XKCD comic regarding Little Bobby Tables should help to illustrate the problem. The input parameter being used directly in a database query is maliciously formed to change the query so that it damages or otherwise exploits the database.

Defeating SQL Injection

When we create our `Gateway` methods, we should never assume the parameter values are safe. It doesn't matter if we expect the parameters to be hard-coded to constant values on every call, or otherwise guaranteed to be safe. At some point, someone is going to change a bit of code that calls the `Gateway` method and we will have a security issue. Instead, we need to treat every parameter value as unsafe, and deal with it accordingly.

Thus, to defeat SQL injection attempts, we should do one of three things with every query in our `Gateway` methods (indeed, in any SQL statement anywhere in the codebase):

1. The best solution is to use prepared statements and parameter binding instead of query string interpolation.

2. The second-best solution is to use the database layer's "quote-and-escape" mechanism on each parameter before interpolating it into the query string.

3. The third-best solution is to escape each of the input parameters before interpolating them into the query string.

> Alternatively, we can avoid the problem of strings entirely by casting expected numeric values to `int` or `float`.

Let's examine the third-best solution first, since it is more likely to already be present in our legacy codebase. We use the database's `escape` functionality to escape each parameter before we use it in a query string, and quote it appropriately for the database. Thus, we can rewrite the `selectAllByPostId()` method like so, assuming a MySQL database:

```php
<?php
2 public function selectAllByPostId($post_id)
3 {
```

```
4 $post_id = "'" . $this->db->escape($post_id) . "'";
5 $stm = "SELECT * FROM comments WHERE post_id = {$post_id}";
6 return $this->db->query($stm);
7 }
8 ?>
```

Escaping values for interpolation into strings is a third-best solution for several reasons. The main one is that the escaping logic is sometimes insufficient. Something like `mysql_escape_string()` function is simply not good enough for our purposes here. Even the `mysql_real_escape_string()` method has a flaw that will allow attackers to succeed at SQL injection attempts depending on the current character set. However, this may be the only option available to the underlying database driver.

The second-best solution is a variation of escaping called quote-and-escape. This feature, available only via the `PDO::quote()` method, is safer than escaping because it additionally wraps the value in quotes and deals with the proper character set automatically. This avoids the character set mismatch issues inherent to just escaping and adding quotes on our own.

A rewritten `selectAllByPostId()` method might look like this with a `Db` object that exposes the `PDO::quote()` method:

```
<?php
2 public function selectAllByPostId($post_id)
3 {
4 $post_id = $this->db->quote($post_id);
5 $stm = "SELECT * FROM comments WHERE post_id = {$post_id}";
6 return $this->db->query($stm);
7 }
8 ?>
```

This is a safe approach when we remember to use it. The issue here, of course, is that if we add a parameter to the method, we may forget to quote it, and then we are vulnerable to SQL injection again.

Finally, the best solution: prepared statements and parameter binding. These are only available via PDO (which works with almost all databases) and the `mysqli` extension. Each has its own variations on how to handle statement preparation. We will use PDO style examples here.

Instead of interpolating values into query strings, we use named placeholders to indicate where parameters should be placed in a query string. We then tell PDO to prepare the string as a `PDOStatement` object, and bind values to the named placeholders when we execute the query through that prepared statement. PDO automatically uses safe representations of the parameter values, making us secure against SQL injection attacks.

Here is an example of what a rewrite would look like using a Db object that exposes the PDO statement preparation logic and execution:

```php
1 <?php
2 public function selectAllByPostId($post_id)
3 {
4 $stm = "SELECT * FROM comments WHERE post_id = :post_id";
5 $bind = array('post_id' => $post_id);
6
7 $sth = $this->db->prepare($stm);
8 $sth->execute($bind);
9 return $sth->fetchAll(PDO::FETCH_ASSOC);
10 }
11 ?>
```

The great benefit here is that we never use the parameter variables in the query string. We always and only use named placeholders, and bind the placeholders to the parameter values into the prepared statement. This idiom makes it clear when we are improperly using interpolated variables, and PDO automatically complains if there are extra or missing bound values, so the chances of accidentally making an insecure change are greatly reduced.

Write a test

Now it is time to write a test for our new class method. The test we write at this point is going to be less perfect than we would like because we need to interact with the database. However, an imperfect test is better than no test. As *The Way Of Testivus* tells us, we write the test we can at the time we can.

The test for our new Gateway method might look something like this:

tests/classes/Domain/Comments/CommentsGatewayTest.php
```php
1 <?php
2 namespace Domain\Comments;
3
4 use Db;
5
6 class CommentsGatewayTest
7 {
8 protected $db;
9
10 protected $gateway;
11
12 public function setUp()
13 {
```

```
14 $this->db = new Db('test_host', 'test_user', 'test_pass');
15 $this->gateway = new CommentsGateway($this->db);
16 }
17
18 public function testSelectAllByPostId()
19 {
20 // a range of known IDs in the comments table
21 $post_id = mt_rand(1,100);
22
23 // get the comment rows
24 $rows = $this->gateway->selectAllByPostId($post_id);
25
26 // make sure they all match the post_id
27 foreach ($rows as $row) {
28 $this->assertEquals($post_id, $row['post_id']);
29 }
30 }
31 }
32 ?>
```

Now we run our test suite to see if the test passes. If it does, we rejoice and move on! If it does not, we continue to refine the `Gateway` method and the related test until both are working properly.

Perfecting Our Tests

As noted earlier, this is very much an imperfect test. Among other things, it depends on a working database connection, and on having data seeded into the database in the first place. By depending on the database, we are dependent on it being in a correct state. If the database does not have the correct data in it, then the test will fail. The failure will come not from the code, which is what we are testing, but from the database, which is mostly beyond our control. One opportunity for improving the test is to change the `Gateway` class to depend on a `DbInterface` instead of a concrete `Db` class. We would then create a `FakeDb` class for testing purposes that implements the `DbInterface`, and inject a `FakeDb` instance into the `Gateway` instead of a real `Db` instance. Doing so would give us greater insight into the correctness of the SQL query string along with greater control over the the data being returned to the `Gateway`. Above all, it would decouple the test from its dependency on a working database. For now, in the interest of expediency, we will use the imperfect test.

Replace the original code

Now that we have a working and tested `Gateway` method, we replace the original code with a call to the `Gateway`. Whereas the old code looked like this:

page_script.php (before)
```
1 <?php
2 $db = new Db($db_host, $db_user, $db_pass);
3 $post_id = $_GET['post_id'];
4 $stm = "SELECT * FROM comments WHERE post_id = $post_id";
5 $rows = $db->query($stm);
6 foreach ($rows as $row) {
7 // output each row
8 }
9 ?>
```

The new version would look like this:

page_script.php (after)
```
1 <?php
2 $db = new Db($db_host, $db_user, $db_pass);
3 $comments_gateway = new CommentsGateway($db);
4 $rows = $comments_gateway->selectAllByPostId($_GET['post_id']);
5 foreach ($rows as $row) {\
6 // output each row
7 }
8 ?>
```

Note that we have done little to modify the operational logic. For example, we have not added error checking that was not previously present. The furthest extent of our modification has been to secure the query against SQL injection via prepared statements.

Test, Commit, Push, Notify QA

As in previous chapters, we now need to spot check the legacy application. Although we have a unit test for the new `Gateway` method, we still need to spot check the part of the application we have modified. If we prepared a characterization test earlier that covers this part of our legacy application, we can run that now. Otherwise, we can do this by browsing to or otherwise invoking the changed part of the application.

Once we are satisfied that we have successfully replaced the embedded SQL with a call to our new `Gateway` method, we commit the changes, including our tests, to revision control. We then push to the central repository and notify the QA team of our changes.

Do ... While

With that complete, we search the codebase again for uses of SQL keywords to indicate embedded query strings. Where they exist outside of a `Gateway` class, we continue extracting the queries to an appropriate `Gateway`. Once all the SQL statements have been moved to `Gateway` classes, we're done.

Common Questions

What about INSERT, UPDATE, and DELETE Statements?

So far we have looked exclusively at `SELECT` statements since they are likely to be the most common case in our legacy codebase. However, there will be a significant number of `INSERT`, `UPDATE`, `DELETE`, and perhaps other statements as well. These are treated essentially the same as the `SELECT` for purposes of extraction to a `Gateway`, but there are some minor differences.

In particular, `INSERT` and `UPDATE` statements may contain a large number of parameters indicating the column values to be inserted or updated. Adding too many parameters to the extracted `Gateway` method signature will make it difficult to work with.

In these cases, we can use a data array to indicate the column names and their corresponding values. We need to make sure that we are inserting or updating only the correct columns, though.

For example, say we start with the following code in a page script to save a new comment with the name of the commenter, the comment body, the IP address of the commenter, and the post ID to which the comment is attached:

page_script.php
```
1 <?php
2 $db = new Db($db_host, $db_user, $db_pass);
3
4 $name = $db->escape($_POST['name']);
5 $body = $db->escape($_POST['body']);
6 $post_id = (int) $_POST['id'];
7 $ip = $db->escape($_SERVER['REMOTE_ADDR']);
8
9 $stm = "INSERT INTO comments (post_id, name, body, ip) "
10 .= "VALUES ($post_id, '{$name}', '{$body}', '{$ip}'";
11
12 $db->query($stm);
13 $comment_id = $db->lastInsertId();
14 ?>
```

When we extract this to a method in our `CommentsGateway`, we could have a parameter for each column value being inserted. In this case there are only four columns, but if there were a dozen, the method signature would be harder to deal with.

As an alternative to one parameter per column, we could pass an array of data as a single parameter and then work with that inside the method. This example of using a data array includes a prepared statement with placeholders to defeat SQL injection attacks:

```php
1 <?php
2 public function insert(array $bind)
3 {
4 $stm = "INSERT INTO comments (post_id, name, body, ip) "
5 .= "VALUES (:post_id, :name, :body, :ip)";
6 $this->db->query($stm, $bind);
7 return $this->db->lastInsertId();
8 }
9 ?>
```

Once we have a method like this in the `CommentsGateway`, we can modify the original code to read more like the following:

page_script.php
```php
1 <?php
2 $db = new Db($db_host, $db_user, $db_pass);
3 $comments_gateway = new CommentsGateway($db);
4
5 $input = array(
6 'name' => $_POST['name'],
7 'body' => $_POST['body'],
8 'post_id' => $_POST['id'],
9 'ip' => $_SERVER['REMOTE_ADDR'],
10 );
11
12 $comment_id = $comments_gateway->insert($input);
13 ?>
```

What about Repetitive SQL strings?

One thing we will probably encounter during this process is a large amount of repetition, or repetition with variation, in the query strings throughout our legacy application.

For example, we may find a comments-related query elsewhere in our legacy application that looks like this:

```
1 <?php
2 $stm = "SELECT * FROM comments WHERE post_id = $post_id LIMIT 10";
3 ?>
```

The query string is identical to the example code from the beginning of this chapter, except it has a LIMIT clause attached. Should we create an entirely new method for this query, or do we modify an existing method?

This is the sort of thing that requires professional judgment and familiarity with the codebase. In this case, modification seems to be reasonable, but in other situations the difference might be great enough to warrant an entirely new method.

If we choose to modify an existing method in the CommentsGateway, we might rewrite selectAllByPostId() to include an optional LIMIT:

```
1 <?php
2 public function selectAllByPostId($post_id, $limit = null)
3 {
4 $stm = "SELECT * FROM comments WHERE post_id = :post_id";
5 if ($limit) {
6 $stm .= " LIMIT " . (int) $limit;
7 }
8 $bind = array('post_id' => $post_id);
9 return $this->db->query($stm, $bind);
10 }
11 ?>
```

Now that we have modified the application class, we need to run our existing tests. If they fail, we rejoice! We have discovered that our change was flawed, and the tests have prevented that bug from making it into production. If they pass, we rejoice, because things are still working the way they used to before the change.

Finally, after the existing tests pass, we modify the CommentsGatewayTest so that it checks to see if the new LIMIT functionality works properly. This test continues to be imperfect, but it gets the point across:

```
tests/classes/Domain/Comments/CommentsGatewayTest.php
1 <?php
2 public function testSelectAllByPostId()
3 {
4 // a range of known IDs in the comments table
5 $post_id = mt_rand(1,100);
6
```

```
 7 // get the comment rows
 8 $rows = $this->gateway->selectAllByPostId($post_id);
 9
10 // make sure they all match the post_id
11 foreach ($rows as $row) {
12 $this->assertEquals($post_id, $row['post_id']);
13 }
14
15 // test with a limit
16 $limit = 10;
17 $rows = $this->gateway->selectAllByPostId($post_id, $limit);
18 $this->assertTrue(count($rows) <= $limit);
19 }
20 }
21 ?>
```

We run the tests yet again to make sure our new LIMIT functionality works, and refine the code and test until it passes.

We then proceed to replace the original embedded SQL code with a call to the Gateway, spot check, commit, and so on.

> We need to be cautious here. After seeing one variation of a query, we will be able to imagine many other possible variations of that query. The resulting temptation will be to preemptively modify our Gateway methods to account for the imagined variations before we actually encounter them. Unless we have actually seen a particular variation in the legacy codebase, we should restrain ourselves from writing code for that variation. We do not want to get too far ahead of what the codebase actually requires right now. The goal is to improve in small steps on a visible path, not to make giant leaps into a fog of imagination.

What about complex query strings?

The examples so far have been relatively simple query strings. These simple examples help to keep the process clear. However, we are likely to see very complicated queries in our legacy codebase. These may include queries built up in pieces, using several conditional statements to modify how the pieces are built, with many different parameters being used in the query. Here is one example of a complex query taken from *Appendix A, Typical Legacy Page Script*:

```
1 <?php
2 // ...
3 define("SEARCHNUM", 10);
4 // ...
```

```
 5 $page = ($page) ? $page : 0;
 6
 7 if (!empty($p) && $p!="all" && $p!="none") {
 8 $where = "`foo` LIKE '%$p%'";
 9 } else {
10 $where = "1";
11 }
12
13 if ($p=="hand") {
14 $where = "`foo` LIKE '%type1%'"
15 . " OR `foo` LIKE '%type2%'"
16 . " OR `foo` LIKE '%type3%'";
17 }
18
19 $where .= " AND `bar`='1'";
20 if ($s) {
21 $s = str_replace(" ", "%", $s);
22 $s = str_replace("'", "", $s);
23 $s = str_replace(";", "", $s);
24 $where .= " AND (`baz` LIKE '%$s%')";
25 $orderby = "ORDER BY `baz` ASC";
26 } elseif ($letter!="none" && $letter) {
27 $where .= " AND (`baz` LIKE '$letter%'"
28 . " OR `baz` LIKE 'The $letter%')";
29 $orderby = "ORDER BY `baz` ASC";
30 } else {
31 $orderby = "ORDER BY `item_date` DESC";
32 }
33 $query = mysql_query(
34 "SELECT * FROM `items` WHERE $where $orderby
35 LIMIT $page,".SEARCHNUM;
36 );
37 ?>
```

For complex arrangements of this sort, we will need to pay great attention to detail in extracting the relevant query-building logic to our Gateway. The main considerations are to determine which variables are used in the query-building logic, and to set those up as parameters to our new Gateway method. We can then move the query-building logic to our Gateway.

A first pass at extracting the embedded SQL-related logic to a `Gateway` method follows:

```php
1 <?php
2 namespace Domain\Items;
3
4 class ItemsGateway
5 {
6 protected $mysql_link;
7
8 public function __construct($mysql_link)
9 {
10 $this->mysql_link = $mysql_link;
11 }
12
13 public function selectAll(
14 $p = null,
15 $s = null,
16 $letter = null,
17 $page = 0,
18 $searchnum = 10
19 ) {
20 if (!empty($p) && $p!="all" && $p!="none") {
21 $where = "`foo` LIKE '%$p%'";
22 } else {
23 $where = "1";
24 }
25
26 if ($p=="hand") {
27 $where = "`foo` LIKE '%type1%'"
28 . " OR `foo` LIKE '%type2%'"
29 . " OR `foo` LIKE '%type3%'";
30 }
31
32 $where .= " AND `bar`='1'";
33 if ($s) {
34 $s = str_replace(" ", "%", $s);
35 $s = str_replace("'", "", $s);
36 $s = str_replace(";", "", $s);
37 $where .= " AND (`baz` LIKE '%$s%')";
38 $orderby = "ORDER BY `baz` ASC";
39 } elseif ($letter!="none" && $letter) {
40 $where .= " AND (`baz` LIKE '$letter%'"
```

```
41 . " OR `baz` LIKE 'The $letter%')";
42 $orderby = "ORDER BY `baz` ASC";
43 } else {
44 $orderby = "ORDER BY `item_date` DESC";
45 }
46
47 $stm = "SELECT *
48 FROM `items`
49 WHERE $where
50 $orderby
51 LIMIT $page, $searchnum";
52
53 return mysql_query($stm, $this->mysql_link);
54 }
55 }
56 ?>
```

Even though we have removed some dependencies (e.g. the implicit global dependency on a `mysql_connect()` link identifier), there are still lots of problems with this first pass. Among other things, it is still vulnerable to SQL injection. We would need to use `mysql_real_escape_string()` on every parameter used in the query, and cast the `LIMIT` values to integers.

Once we complete the extraction and its related test, we change the original code to something like this:

```
1 <?php
2 // ...
3 define("SEARCHNUM", 10);
4 // ...
5 $page = ($page) ? $page : 0;
6 $mysql_link = mysql_connect($db_host, $db_user, $db_pass);
7 $items_gateway = new \Domain\Items\ItemsGateway($mysql_link);
8 $query = $items_gateway->selectAll($p, $s, $letter, $page,
SEARCHNUM);
9 ?>
```

What about queries inside non-Gateway classes?

The examples in this chapter show SQL query strings embedded in page scripts. It is just as likely that we will find query strings embedded in non-Gateway classes as well.

In these cases, we follow the same process as we did for page scripts. One added issue is that we will have to pass the `Gateway` dependency to the class. For example, say we have a `Foo` class that uses a `doSomething()` method to retrieve comments:

```php
1 <?php
2 class Foo
3 {
4 protected $db;
5
6 public function __construct(Db $db)
7 {
8 $this->db = $db;
9 }
10
11 public function doSomething($post_id)
12 {
13 $stm = "SELECT * FROM comments WHERE post_id = $post_id";
14 $rows = $this->db->query($stm);
15 foreach ($rows as $row) {
16 // do something with each row
17 }
18 return $rows;
19 }
20 }
21 ?>
```

We extract the SQL query string and its related logic as we did with the page script. We then modify the `Foo` class to take the `Gateway` as a dependency instead of the `Db` object, and use the `Gateway` as needed:

```php
1 <?php
2 use Domain\Comments\CommentsGateway;
3
4 class Foo
5 {
6 protected $comments_gateway;
7
8 public function __construct(CommentsGateway $comments_gateway)
9 {
```

```
10 $this->comments_gateway = $comments_gateway;
11 }
12
13 public function doSomething($post_id)
14 {
15 $rows = $this->comments_gateway->selectAllByPostId($post_id);
16 foreach ($rows as $row) {
17 // do something with each row
18 }
19 return $rows;
20 }
21 }
22 ?>
```

Can we extend from a base Gateway class?

If we have many Gateway classes that all have similar functionality, it may be reasonable to collect some of that functionality into an AbstractGateway. For example, if they all need the a Db connection, and all have similar select*() methods, we might do something like the following:

```
classes/AbstractGateway.php
1 <?php
2 abstract class AbstractGateway
3 {
4 protected $table;
5
6 protected $primary_key;
7
8 public function __construct(Db $db)
9 {
10 $this->db = $db;
11 }
12
13 public function selectOneByPrimaryKey($primary_val)
14 {
15 $stm = "SELECT * FROM {$this->table} "
16 .= "WHERE {$this->primary_key} = :primary_val";
17 $bind = array('primary_val' => $primary_val);
18 return $this->db->query($stm, $bind);
19 }
20 }
21 ?>
```

We can then extend a class from that base `AbstractGateway` and tune the extended properties for a specific table:

```php
1 <?php
2 namespace Domain\Items;
3
4 class ItemsGateway extends \AbstractGateway
5 {
6 protected $table = 'items';
7 protected $primary_key = 'item_id';
8 }
9 ?>
```

The base `selectOneByPrimaryKey()` method can then work with a wide range of `Gateway` classes. We can still add other concrete methods on specific `Gateway` classes as needed.

> Be cautious with this approach. We should abstract only the functionality that already exists in the behaviors we have already extracted. Resist the temptation to preemptively create functionality that we have not actually seen in the legacy codebase.

What about multiple queries and complex result structures?

The examples in this chapter have shown single queries against single tables. It is likely that we will encounter logic that uses multiple queries against several different tables and then combines the results into a complex domain entity or collection. Here is an example:

```php
1 <?php
2 // build a structure of posts with author and statistics data,
3 // with all comments on each post.
4 $page = (int) $_GET['page'];
5 $limit = 10;
6 $offset = $page * $limit; // a zero-based paging system
7 $stm = "SELECT *
8 FROM posts
9 LEFT JOIN authors ON authors.id = posts.author_id
10 LEFT JOIN stats ON stats.post_id = posts.id
11 LIMIT {$limit} OFFSET {$offset}"
12 $posts = $db->query($stm);
13
```

```
14 foreach ($posts as &$post) {
15 $stm = "SELECT * FROM comments WHERE post_id = {$post['id']}";
16 $post['comments'] = $db->query($stm);
17 }
18 ?>
```

> This example shows a classic N+1 problem where one query is issued for each member of a master set. The first query to get the blog posts will be followed by 10 more queries, one for each blog post, to get the comments. The total number of queries is thus 10, plus one for the initial query. For 50 posts, there would be 51 queries total. This is a typical source of performance drags in legacy applications. For extended discussion of, and solutions to, the N+1 problem, please see *Solving The N+1 Problem in PHP* (https://leanpub.com/sn1php)

The first issue is to identify how we can split up the queries into `Gateway` methods. Some queries will have to go together, while others can be separated. In this case, the first and second queries can be separated into different `Gateway` classes and methods.

The next issue is to determine which `Gateway` class should receive the extracted logic. This can sometimes be hard to figure out when multiple tables are involved, so we have to choose which is the primary subject of the query. The first query above references posts, authors, and stats, but it seems clear from the logic that we are primarily interested in the posts.

As such, we can extract the first query to a `PostsGateway`. We want to modify the query itself as little as possible, so we leave the joins and such in place:

```
1 <?php
2 namespace Domain\Posts;
3
4 class PostsGateway
5 {
6 protected $db;
7
8 public function __construct(Db $db)
9 {
10 $this->db = $db;
11 }
12
13 public function selectAllWithAuthorsAndStats($limit = null, $offset = null)
14 {
```

```
15 $limit = (int) $limit;
```
https://leanpub.com/sn1php
```
16 $offset = (int) $offset;
17 $stm = "SELECT *
18 FROM posts
19 LEFT JOIN authors ON authors.id = posts.author_id
20 LEFT JOIN stats ON stats.post_id = posts.id
21 LIMIT {$limit} OFFSET {$offset}"
22 return $this->db->query($stm);
23 }
24 }
25 ?>
```

Once completed, we proceed to write a test for the new functionality based on the first query. We modify the code and test until the test passes.

The second query, the one related to comments, is the same as our earlier example.

After we finish the extractions and their related tests, we can modify the page script to look like the following:

```
1 <?php
2 $db = new Database($db_host, $db_user, $db_pass);
3 $posts_gateway = new \Domain\Posts\PostsGateway($db);
4 $comments_gateway = new \Domain\Comments\CommentsGateway($db);
5
6 // build a structure of posts with author and statistics data,
7 // with all comments on each post.
8 $page = (int) $_GET['page'];
9 $limit = 10;
10 $offset = $page * $limit; // a zero-based paging system
11 $posts = $posts_gateway->selectAllWithAuthorsAndStats($limit,
$offset);
12
13 foreach ($posts as &$post) {
14 $post['comments'] = $comments_gateway->selectAllByPostId($post['
id']);
15 }
16 ?>
```

What if there is no Database Class?

Many legacy codebases do not have a database access layer. Instead, these legacy applications use the `mysql` extension directly in their page scripts. Calls to `mysql` functions are scattered throughout the codebase and are not gathered into a single class.

If we can upgrade to PDO, we should. However, it may not be possible to upgrade away from `mysql` for various reasons. PDO does not work quite the same way as `mysql`, and changing from `mysql` idioms to PDO ones might be too much to do in a single step. A migration at this point might also make testing more difficult than we would like.

On the other hand, we could move the `mysql` calls as they are into our `Gateway` classes. Doing so seems reasonable at first. However, the `mysql` extension has a bit of global state built into it. Any `mysql` functions that need a link identifer (i.e., a server connection) automatically use the most-recent connection resource when no link identifier is passed. This is counter to the principles of dependency injection, since we would rather not be dependent on global state if we can help it.

Thus, instead of migrating directly to PDO, and instead of leaving the `msyql` function calls as they are, I suggest we wrap the `mysql` calls in a class that proxies method calls to the `mysql` functions. We can then use the class methods instead of the `mysql` functions. The class itself can contain the link identifier and pass it to each method call. This will give us a database access layer that our `Gateway` objects can use without changing the `mysql` idiomatic usage too greatly.

One operational example implementation of such a wrapper is the `MysqlDatabase` class. When we create an instance of `MysqlDatabase`, it retains the connection information but does not actually connect to the server. It only connects when we call a method that actually needs a server connection. This lazy-loading approach helps us reduce resource usage. In addition, the `MysqlDatabase` class explicitly adds the link identifier argument, which is optional in the relevant `mysql` functions, so that we are never dependent on the implicit global state of the `mysql` extension.

To replace `mysql` function calls with `MysqlDatabase` calls:

1. Search the entire codebase for the `mysql_` prefix on function calls.

2. In each file where there are function calls with the `mysql_` function prefix ...

   ° Create or inject an instance of `MysqlDatabase`.

   ° Replace each `mysql_` function prefix with the `MysqlDatabase` object variable and a single arrow operator (`->`). If we are sticklers for style, we can can convert the remaining method name portion from `snake_case()` to `camelCase()` as well.

3. Spot check, commit, push, and notify QA.

4. Continue searching for the `mysql_` prefix on function calls until they have all been replaced with `MysqlDatabase` method calls.

For example, say we have a piece of legacy code like this:

Using mysql functions

```
1 <?php
2 mysql_connect($db_host, $db_user, $db_pass);
3 mysql_select_db('my_database');
4 $result = mysql_query('SELECT * FROM table_name LIMIT 10');
5 while ($row = mysql_fetch_assoc($result)) {
6 // do something with each row
7 }
8 ?>
```

Using the above process, we can convert the code to use the `MysqlDatabase` object instead:

Using the MysqlDatabase class

```
1 <?php
2 $db = new \Mlaphp\MysqlDatabase($db_host, $db_user, $db_pass);
3 $db->select_db('my_database'); // or $db->selectDb('my_database')
4 $result = $db->query('SELECT * FROM table_name LIMIT 10');
5 while ($row = $db->fetch_assoc($result)) {
6 // do something with each row
7 }
8 ?>
```

That code, in turn, can be extracted to a `Gateway` class using an injected `MysqlDatabase` object.

> For our page scripts, it may be best to create a `MysqlDatabase` instance in our existing setup file and use that, instead of creating one separately in each page script. The lazy-connecting nature of the implementation means that if we never make a call to the database, no connection will ever be made, so we don't need to worry about unnecessary resource usage. The existing legacy codebase will help us determine if this is a reasonable approach.

Once our `Gateway` classes use an injected `MysqlDatabase` object, we can then proceed to planning a migration away from the wrapped `mysql` functions over to `PDO` with its different idioms and usage. Because the database access logic is now wrapped by `Gateway` objects, the migration and testing will be easier than if we had replaced `mysql` calls spread throughout the codebase.

Review and next steps

When we have completed this step, all of our SQL statements will be inside `Gateway` classes, and no longer in our page scripts or other non-Gateway classes. We will also have tests for our `Gateway` classes.

From here on out, any time we need to add new calls to the database, we will do so only in the `Gateway` classes. Any time we need to fetch or save data, we will use the `Gateway` methods instead of writing embedded SQL. This gives us a clear separation of concerns between the database interactions and our future model layer and entity objects.

Now that we have separated our database interactions into their own layer, we are going to inspect all the calls to the `Gateway` objects throughout the legacy application. We will examine how the returned results are manipulated by the page scripts and other classes, and begin extracting the behaviors that define our model layer.

9
Extract Domain Logic to Transactions

In the previous chapter, we extracted all our SQL statements to a layer of *Gateway* objects. This encapsulates the interactions between the application and the database.

However, we usually need to apply some amount of business or domain logic to the data coming from and going back to the database. The logic can include things like data validation, adding or modifying values for presentation or calculation purposes, collecting simpler records into more complex ones, using the data to perform related actions, and so on. This domain logic is often embedded into a page script, making that logic difficult to reuse and test.

This chapter describes one way to extract domain behaviors into a separate layer. In many ways, this chapter forms the very core of the book: everything before now has led us to this central concern of the legacy application, and everything that comes after will lead us into layers above and around this core functionality.

Domain or Model?

The domain logic in the legacy application is the model portion of model-view-controller. However, the legacy codebase is unlikely to have separate entity objects that provide a full model of the business domain. Thus, we will be speaking in terms of domain logic and not model logic throughout this chapter. If we are lucky enough to have separate model objects already, so much the better.

Embedded Domain Logic

Although we have extracted SQL statements, the page scripts and classes are probably manipulating the results and performing other actions related to the retrieved data. These manipulations and actions are the core of the domain logic, and it is currently embedded along with other non-domain concerns.

We can see an example of the progression from embedded SQL to using *Gateway* classes by examining the differences between the code in *Appendix B, Code before Gateway* and *Appendix C, Code after Gateway*. The code is too lengthy to present here. What we want to notice is that even after extracting the embedded SQL statements, the code is still doing a lot of work with the incoming and outgoing data before the results are presented to the user.

Having the domain logic embedded in the page script makes it very difficult to test that logic in isolation. We also cannot reuse it easily. If we wanted to search for repetition and duplication in how we work with the domain entities (in this case a series of articles) we would need to review every page script in the entire application.

The solution here is to extract the domain logic to one or more classes so that we can test them independently of any particular page script. We can then instantiate the domain logic classes and use them in any page script we like.

Before we can apply that solution, we need to determine how to structure the target classes for our domain logic.

Domain logic patterns

Martin Fowler's **Patterns of Enterprise Application Architecture (PoEAA)** catalogs four domain logic patterns:

- **Transaction Script**: It organizes [domain] logic primarily as a single procedure, making calls directly to the database or through a thin database wrapper. Each transaction will have its own Transaction Script, although common subtasks can be broken into subprocedures."

- **Domain Model**: It creates a web of interconnected objects, where each object represents some meaningful individual, whether as large as a corporation or as small as a single line on an order form.

- **Table Module**: It organizes domain logic with one class per table in the database, and a single instance of a class contains the various procedures that will act on the data, if you have many orders, a Domain Model will have one order object per order while a Table Module will have one object to handle all orders.

- **Service Layer**: It defines an application's boundary and its set of available operations from the perspective of interfacing client layers. It encapsulates the application's business logic, controlling transactions and coordinating responses in the implementation of its operations.

> I strongly recommend purchasing PoEAA in hard copy and reading the pattern descriptions and examples in full. The book is an absolute must-have reference for the professional programmer. I find myself consulting it on a weekly basis (sometimes more often) and it always provides clarity and insight.

The choice before us now is this: given the existing structure of our legacy application, which of these patterns best fits the architecture currently in place?

We will dismiss Service Layer at this point, since it implies a level of sophistication that is probably not present in our legacy application. We will likewise dismiss Domain Model, since it implies a well-designed set of business entity objects that encapsulate behavior. If the legacy application already has one of these patterns implemented, then so much the better. Otherwise, that leaves us with the Table Module and Transaction Script patterns.

When we extracted our SQL statements to `Gateway` classes in the previous chapter, those `Gateway` classes were likely to follow the Table Data Gateway pattern, in particular if they were simple enough to interact with only a single table per `Gateway` class. This makes it seem like the Table Module pattern would be a good fit for our domain logic.

However, it is unlikely that each remaining page script or class with embedded domain logic is interacting with a single table at a time. More frequently, legacy applications have many interactions across many tables in a single class or script. As such, we will begin by using the Transaction Script pattern when we extract our domain logic.

Transaction Script is admittedly a simple pattern to follow. With it, we extract the domain logic from the page script and dump it into a class method mostly intact. We make modifications to the logic only for getting data into and out of the class method so that the original code can still operate properly.

Although we may wish for something more sophisticated than Transaction Script, we have to remember that one of our goals here is to avoid changing the existing logic too dramatically. We are refactoring, not rewriting. What we want right now is to move the code around so that it can be tested and reused appropriately. Thus, a Transaction Script is probably the best way to wrap our legacy domain logic as-it-exists, not as-we-want-it-to-be.

Once we extract the domain logic to its own layer, we will then be able to see that logic more clearly and with less distraction. At that point, if it is truly needed, we can begin to plan a refactoring of the domain layer to something more sophisticated. For example, we may build a Service Layer that uses Table Modules or a Domain Model to coordinate the various domain interactions. The interface presented to the page scripts by the Service Layer might remain completely unchanged from the Transaction Script interface, although the underlying architecture may have changed completely. But that is a task for another day.

> **What about Active Record?**
>
> Ruby on Rails is famous for using the Active Record pattern, and many PHP developers love that kind of database interaction. It definitely has its strengths. However, Fowler classifies Active Record as a data source architecture pattern, not a domain logic pattern, so we will not be addressing it here.

The Extraction Process

Of the refactoring processes described in this book, extracting domain logic is going to be the most difficult, time consuming, and detail-oriented. This is a very tough thing to do, and it requires a lot of care and attention. The domain logic is the very core of our legacy application, and we need to make sure to pull out just the right parts. This means success is completely dependent on our familiarity and competence with the the legacy application as it exists now.

Luckily, our prior exercises in modernizing our legacy codebase have given us a broad overview of the application as a whole, as well as deep knowledge of the specific parts we have had to extract and refactor. This should endow us with the confidence to complete this task successfully. It is a demanding, but ultimately satisfying, activity.

In general, we proceed as follows:

1. Search the entire codebase for uses of `Gateway` classes that exist outside `Transactions` classes.

2. Where we find `Gateway` usage, examine the logic surrounding the `Gateway` operations to discover which portions of that logic are related to the domain behaviors of the application.

3. Extract the relevant domain logic to one or more `Transactions` classes related to the domain elements, and modify the original code to use the `Transactions` class instead of the embedded domain logic.

4. Spot check to make sure the original code still works properly, and modify the extracted logic as necessary to ensure correct operation.

5. Write tests for the extracted `Transactions` logic, refining them along with the tested code until they pass.

6. When all original tests and new tests pass, commit the code and tests, push to the common repository, and notify QA.

7. Search again for uses of `Gateway` classes, and continue extracting domain logic until `Gateway` usage exists only in `Transactions`.

Search for uses of Gateway

As in earlier chapters, we use our project-wide search facility to find where we create new instances of `Gateway` classes:

Search for:

```
new .*Gateway
```

The new `Gateway` instance may be used directly in a page script, in which case we have found some candidate code for extracting domain logic. If the `Gateway` instance is injected into a class, we now need to dive into that class to find where the `Gateway` is used. The code surrounding that usage will be our candidate for extracting domain logic.

Discover and Extract Relevant Domain Logic

> When extracting logic to a class method, we should be careful to follow all the lessons we learned about dependency injection in prior chapters. Among other things, this means: no use of globals, replacing superglobals with a `Request` object, no use of the new keyword outside `Factory` classes, and (of course) injecting objects via the constructor as needed.

After we have found some candidate code using a `Gateway`, we need to examine the code surrounding `Gateway` usage for these and other operations:

- Normalizing, filtering, sanitizing, and validating of data
- Calculation, modification, creation, and manipulation of data
- Sequential or concurrent operations and actions using the data
- Retention of success/failure/warning/notice messages from those operations and actions
- Retention of values and variables for later inputs and outputs

These and other pieces of logic are likely to be domain-related.

To successfully extract the domain logic to one or more `Transactions` classes and methods, we will have to perform these and other activities:

- Breaking up or reorganizing the extracted domain logic into support methods

- Breaking up or reorganizing the original code to wrap around the new `Transactions` calls

- Retaining, returning, or reporting data needed by the original code

- Adding, changing, or removing variables in the original code related to the extracted domain logic

- Creating and injecting dependencies for the `Transactions` classes and methods

> Discovery-and-extraction is best thought of as a learning exercise. Picking apart the legacy application like this is a way of learning how the application is constructed. As such, we should not be afraid to make multiple attempts at extraction. If our first attempt fails, ends up ugly, or gives poor results, we should feel no guilt about scrapping the work and starting over, having learned a little more about what works and what doesn't. For my own part, I often make two or three passes at extracting domain logic before the work is completed to my satisfaction. This is where a revision control system makes our life so much easier; we can work piecemeal, committing only as we are happy with the result, and reverting back to earlier stages if we need to begin again from a clean slate.

Example Extraction

By way of example, recall the code we started with in *Appendix B, Code before Gateways*. Earlier in this chapter we mentioned that we had extracted embedded SQL statements to *ArticlesGateway* classes, ending up with the code in *Appendix C, Code after Gateways*. We now go from that to *Appendix D, Code after Transaction Scripts* where we have extracted the domain logic to an `ArticleTransactions` class.

The extracted domain logic does not appear particularly complicated in its completed form, but actually doing the work turns out to be quite detailed. Review the *Appendix C, Code after Gateways* and compare to the *Appendix D, Code after Transaction Scripts*. Among other things, we should find the following:

- We discovered two separate transactions being performed in the page script: one to submit a new article, and one to update an existing article. In turn, these each needed to operate on the user's credit counts in the database, along with various data normalizing and support operations.

- We extracted the relevant domain logic to an `ArticleTransactions` class and two separate methods, one for creating and one for updating. We named the `ArticleTransactions` methods for the domain logic being performed, not for the implemenation of the underlying technical operations.

- Input filtering has been encapsulated as a support method in the `ArticleTransactions` class for reuse across both of the transaction methods.

- The new `ArticleTransactions` class receives `ArticlesGateway` and `UsersGateway` dependencies to manage the database interactions instead of making direct SQL calls.

- Several variables that were related only to the domain logic have been removed from the page script and placed into the `Transactions` class as properties.

- The code in the original page script has been greatly reduced. It is now essentially an object creation and injection mechanism, passing user inputs to the domain layer and getting back data to output later.

- Because the domain logic is now encapsulated, the original code can no longer see the `$failure` variable as it gets modified throughout the transaction. That code must now get failure information from the `ArticleTransactions` class for later presentation.

After the extraction, we have a `classes/` directory structure that looks something like the following. This is a result of using a domain-oriented class structure when we extracted SQL to `Gateway` classes:

```
/path/to/app/classes/
1 Domain/
2   Articles/
3     ArticlesGateway.php
4     ArticleTransactions.php
5   Users/
6     UsersGateway.php
```

This need not be our final refactoring. Further modifications of the `ArticleTransactions` are still possible. For example, instead of injecting a `UsersGateway`, it might make sense to extract various domain logic related to users into a `UserTransactions` class and inject that instead. There is still a lot of repetition between the `Transactions` methods. We also need better error checking and condition reporting in the `Transactions` methods. These and other refactorings are secondary, and will be both more noticeable and easier to deal with only after the primary extraction of domain logic.

Spot check the remaining original code

Once we have extracted one or more *Transactions* from the original code, we need to make sure the original code works when using the *Transactions* instead of the embedded domain logic. As before, we do this by running our pre-existing characterization tests. If we do not have characterization tests, we must browse to or otherwise invoke the changed code. If these tests fail, we rejoice! We have discovered that the extraction was flawed, and we have a chance to fix it before we deploy to production. If the "tests" pass, we likewise rejoice, and move on.

Write tests for the extracted transactions

We now know the original code works with the newly extracted *Transactions* logic. However, the new classes and methods need their own set of tests. As with everything else related to extracting domain logic, writing these tests is likely to be detailed and demanding. The logic is probably convoluted, with lots of branches and loops. We should not let this deter us from testing. At the very least, we need to write tests that cover the main cases of the domain logic.

If necessary, we may refactor the extracted logic to separate methods that are themselves more easily testable. Breaking up the extracted logic will make it easier for us to see the flow and find repeated elements of logic. We must remember, though, that our goal is to maintain the existing behavior, not change the behavior presented by the legacy application.

For insights and techniques on how to make the extracted logic more testable, please see *Refactoring* (http://refactoring.com/)by Martin Fowler et al., as well as *Working Effectively With Legacy Code* (https://www.amazon.com/Working-Effectively-Legacy-Michael-Feathers/dp/0131177052)by Michael Feathers.

Spot check again, Commit, Push, Notify QA

Finally, because our testing and related refactoring of the extracted *Transactions* logic may have introduced some unexpected changes, we spot check the original code one more time using our characterization tests or by otherwise invoking the relevant code. If these fail, we rejoice! We have found out that our changes were not as good as we thought, and we have a chance to correct the code and tests before they get too far away from us.

When both the original code tests and the extracted *Transactions* tests pass, we rejoice again! We can now commit all of our new work, push it to the central repository, and notify QA that our modernized code is ready for them to review.

Do ... While

We begin the extraction process over again by looking for another *Gateway* usage outside a *Transactions* class. We continue extracting and testing until all *Gateway* calls occur inside *Transactions* classes.

Common Questions

Are we talking about SQL transactions?

The term Transaction Script refers to an architectural pattern, and does not mean the the domain logic must be wrapped in an SQL transaction. It is easy to confuse the two ideas.

Having said that, keeping SQL transactions in mind may help us when extracting domain logic. One useful rule-of-thumb is that pieces of domain logic should be split up according to how well they would fit inside a single SQL transaction. That hypothetical transaction would be committed, or rolled back, as an atomic whole.

This singularity-of-purpose will help us determine where the boundaries of our domain logic lie. We do not actually add SQL transactions, it is just that thinking in those terms can give us some insight as to the boundaries of the domain logic.

What about repeated Domain Logic?

When we extracted SQL statements to `Gateway` classes, we sometimes found queries that were similar but not exactly identical. We had to determine if there was a way to combine them into a single method or not.

In the same way, we may discover that some parts of our legacy domain logic have been copied and pasted in two or more locations. When we find these, we have the same problem as with our `Gateway` classes. Are the pieces of logic similar enough to be combined into a single method, or must they be different methods (or even in completely different `Transactions`)?

The answer here is it depends. In some cases the repeated code will be an obvious copy of logic elsewhere, meaning we can reuse existing `Transactions` methods. If not, we need to extract to a new `Transactions` class or method.

There is also a middle path, where the domain logic as a whole is different, but there are support elements of logic that are identical across different `Transactions`. In these cases, we can refactor the supporting logic as methods on an abstract base `Transactions` class, and then extend new `Transactions` from it. Alternatively, we can extract the logic to a supporting class and inject it into our `Transactions`.

Are printing and echoing part of Domain Logic?

Our `Transactions` classes should not be using `print` or `echo`. The domain logic should only return or retain data.

When we discover output generation in the middle of our domain logic, we should extract that portion so that it lies outside of the domain logic. In general, this means collecting output in the `Transactions` class and then either returning it or making it available by a separate method. Leave output generation for the presentation layer.

Can a transaction be a class instead of a Method?

In the examples, we showed *Transactions* as a collection of methods related to a particular domain entity, such as *ArticleTransactions*. Each part of the domain logic related to that entity was wrapped in a class method.

However, it is also reasonable to break up domain logic into a one-class-per-transaction structure. Indeed, some transactions may be complex enough that they truly require their own separate classes. There is nothing wrong with using a single class to represent a single domain logic transaction.

For example, the earlier *ArticleTransactions* class might be split into an abstract base class with support methods, and two concrete classes for each of the extracted pieces of domain logic. Each of the concrete classes extends the *AbstractArticleTransaction*, like so:

```
classes/
1 Domain/
2 Articles/
```

```
3 ArticlesGateway.php
4 Transaction/
5 AbstractArticleTransaction.php
6 SubmitNewArticleTransaction.php
7 UpdateExistingArticleTransaction.php
8 Users/
9 UsersGateway.php
```

If we use a one-class-per-transaction approach, what do we name the main method on the single-transaction class, the one that actually performs the transaction? If there is a common convention for main methods that already exist in our legacy codebase, we should adhere to that convention. Otherwise, we need to pick a single consistent method name. Personally, I enjoy co-opting the `__invoke()` magic method for this purpose, but you may wish to use `exec()` or some other appropriate term to indicate we are executing or otherwise performing the transaction.

What about Domain Logic in Gateway classes?

When we extracted our SQL statements to `Gateway` classes, it is possible that we moved some domain logic into them instead of leaving that logic in its original location. At that earlier point in our refactoring work, it was very easy to confuse domain-level input filtering (which makes sure the data conforms to a domain-specific state) with database-level filtering (which makes sure the data is safe to use with the database).

Now we can more easily tell the difference between the two. If we discover that there is domain-level logic in our `Gateway` classes, we should probably extract it to our `Transactions` classes instead. We need to be sure to update the relevant tests as well.

What about Domain logic embedded in Non-Domain classes?

The examples in this chapter show domain logic embedded in page scripts. It is just as likely that we have domain logic embedded in classes as well. If the class can reasonably be considered part of the domain, and contains only domain-related logic, but is not named for the domain, it may be wise to move the class into the domain namespace.

Otherwise, if the class has any responsibilities other than domain logic, we may proceed to extract the domain logic from it in the same way that we extracted logic from a page script. After the extraction, the original class will then need to have the relevant `Transactions` class injected as a dependency. The original class should then make calls to the `Transactions` as appropriate.

Review and next steps

At this point we have extracted the core of our legacy codebase, the domain logic that sits at the center our application, to its own separate and testable layer. This has been the most demanding of the steps in our modernization process, but it has been very much worth our time. We have not made many modifications or improvements to the domain logic itself. Any changes we have made have been just enough to get data into our new `Transactions` classes and then out again for later use.

In a lot of ways, all we have done is shuffle the logic around so that it is independently addressable. Although the domain logic itself may still have many problems, those problems are now *testable* problems. We can continue adding tests as needed to explore edge cases in our domain logic. If we need to add new domain logic, we can create or modify our `Transactions` classes and methods to encapsulate and test that logic.

The process of extracting domain logic to its own layer leaves us with a great foundation for further iterative refactoring of the domain model. If we choose to pursue it, that refactoring will lead us to a more appropriate architecture for the application domain logic. However, what that architecture will be depends on the application. For more information on developing a good domain model for our application, please read *Domain Driven Design* (`https://www.amazon.com/Domain-Driven-Design-Tackling-Complexity-Software/dp/0321125215`)by Eric Evans.

With the extraction of our domain logic to its own layer, we can continue on to the next phase of our modernization process. At this point there are only a few concerns remaining in our original code. Of those concerns, we will next address the presentation layer.

10
Extract Presentation Logic to View Files

When it comes to page scripts in legacy applications, it is very common to see business logic intertwined with presentation logic. For example, the page script does some setup work, then includes a header template, makes a call to the database, outputs the results, calculates some values, prints the calculated values, writes the values back to the database, and includes a footer template.

We have made some steps toward decoupling these concerns by extracting a domain layer for our legacy application. However, calls to the domain layer and other business logic within the page scripts are still mixed in with the presentation logic. Among other things, this intermingling of concerns makes it difficult to test the different aspects of our legacy application.

In this chapter, we will separate all of our presentation logic to its own layer so we can test it separately from our business logic.

Embedded presentation logic

For an example of embedded presentation logic, we can take a look at *Appendix E, Code before Collecting*.

Presentation Logic. The code shows a page script that has been refactored to use domain *Transactions*, but it still has some presentation logic entangled within the rest of the code.

> **What Is The Difference Between Presentation and Business Logic?**
>
> For our purposes, presentation logic includes any and all code that generates output sent to the user (such as a browser or mobile client). This includes not only `echo` and `print` but also `header()` and `setcookie()`. Each of these generates some form of output. "Business logic," on the other hand, is everything else.

The key to decoupling the presentation logic from the business logic is to put the code for them into separate scopes. The script should first perform all of the business logic, then pass the results over to the presentation logic. When that is complete, we will be able to test our presentation logic separately from our business logic.

To achieve this separation of scope, we will move toward using a `Response` object in our page scripts. All of our presentation logic will be executed from within a `Response` instance, instead of directly in the page script. Doing so will provide the scope separation that we need to decouple all output generation, including HTTP headers and cookies, from the rest of the page script.

> **Why A Response Object?**
>
> Often, when we think of presentation, we think of a view or a template system that renders content for us. However, these kinds of systems do not usually encapsulate the full set of output that will be sent to the user. We need to output not just HTTP bodies, but HTTP headers as well. In addition, we need to be able to test that the correct headers have been set, and that the content has been generated properly. As such, the `Response` object is a better fit at this point than a view or template system alone. For our `Response` object, we will use the class provided at `http://mlaphp.com/code`. Note that we will be including files within a *Response* context, which means that the methods on that object will be available to `include` files running "inside" that object.

The Extraction process

Extracting presentation logic is not as difficult as extracting domain logic. However, it does require careful attention and lots of testing along the way.

In general, the process is as follows:

1. Find a page script that contains presentation logic mixed in with the rest of the code.

2. In that script, rearrange the code to collect all presentation logic into a single block *after* all the other logic in the file, then spot check the rearranged code.

3. Extract the block of presentation logic to a view file to be delivered via a `Response`, and spot check the script again to make sure the script works correctly with the new `Response`.

4. Add proper escaping to the presentation logic and spot check again.

5. Commit the new code, push to the common repository, and notify QA.

6. Begin again with the next page script that contains presentation logic mixed in with other non-presentation code.

Search for Embedded presentation logic

In general, it should be easy for us to find presentation logic in our legacy application. At this point we should be familiar enough with the codebase to have a good idea where the page scripts generate output.

If we need a jump-start, we can use our project-wide search facility to find all occurrences of `echo`, `print`, `printf`, `header`, `setcookie`, and `setrawcookie`. Some of these may occur in class methods; we will address that at a later point. For now, we will concentrate on page scripts where these calls occur.

Rearrange the Page script and Spot Check

Now that we have a candidate page script, we need to rearrange the code so there is a clear demarcation between the presentation logic and everything else. For our example here, we will use the code in *Appendix E, Code before Collecting*.

First, we go to the bottom of the file and add a `/* PRESENTATION */` comment as the final line. We then go back to the top of the file. Working line-by-line and block-by-block, we move all presentation logic to the end of the file after our `/* PRESENTATION */` comment. When we are done, the part before the `/* PRESENTATION */` comment should consist only of business logic, and the part after should consist only of presentation logic.

Given our starting code in *Appendix E, Code before Collecting*, we should end up with something more like the code in *Appendix F, Code after Collecting*. In particular, note that we have the following:

- Moved variables not used by the business logic, such as `$current_page`, down the presentation block
- Moved the `header.php` include down to the presentation block
- Moved logic and conditions acting only on presentation variables, such as the `if` that sets the `$page_title`, to the presentation block

- Replaced `$_SERVER['PHP_SELF']` with an `$action` variable
- Replaced `$_GET['id']` with an `$id` variable

> When creating the presentation block, we should be careful to follow all the lessons we learned from earlier chapters about dependency injection. Even though the presentation code is a block within a file (not a class) we should treat the block as if it is a class method. Among other things, this means no use of globals, superglobals, or the new keyword. This will make things easier on us when we extract the presentation block to a view file later.

Now that we have rearranged the page script so that all presentation logic is collected at the end, we need to spot check to make sure the page script still works properly. As usual, we do this by running our pre-existing characterization tests, if we have any. If not, we must browse to or otherwise invoke the changed code.

If the page does not generate the same output as before, our rearrangement has changed the logic somehow. We need to undo and redo the rearrangement until the page works as it should.

Once our spot check is successful, we may wish to commit our changes so far. If our next set of changes goes badly, we can revert the code to this point as a known working state.

Extract Presentation to View file and Spot Check

Now that we have a working page script with all the presentation logic in a single block, we will extract that entire block to its own file, and then use a `Response` to execute the extracted logic.

Create a views/ Directory

First, we need a place to put view files in our legacy application. While I prefer to keep presentation logic near the business logic, that kind of arrangement will make trouble for us in later modernization steps. As such, we will create a new directory in our legacy application called `views/` and place our view files there. This directory should be at the same level as our `classes/` and `tests/` directories. For example:

```
/path/to/app/
1 classes/
2 tests/
3 views/
```

Pick a View File name

Now that we have a place to save our view files, we need to pick a file name for the presentation logic we are about to extract. The view file should be named for the page script, in a path under `views/` that matches the page script path. For example, if we are extracting presentation from a page script at `/foo/bar/baz.php`, the target view file should be saved at `/views/foo/bar/baz.php`.

Sometimes it is useful to use an extension other than just `.php` for our view files. I have found it can be helpful to use an extension that indicates the view format. For example, a view that generates HTML may end in `.html.php`, while a view that generates JSON may end in `.json.php`.

Move Presentation Block to View file

Next, we cut the presentation block from the page script, and paste it into our new view file as-is.

Then, in place of the original presentation block in the page script, we create a `Response` object in our page script and point it to our view file with `setView()`. We also set up an empty call to `setVars()` for later, and finally call the `send()` method.

> We should *always* use the same variable name for the *Response* object in all of our page scripts. All the examples here will use the name `$response`. This is not because the name `$response` is special, but because this level of consistency will be very important in a later chapter.

For example:

```
foo/bar/baz.php
1 <?php
2 // ... business logic ...
3
4 /* PRESENTATION */
5 $response = new \Mlaphp\Response('/path/to/app/views');
6 $response->setView('foo/bar/baz.html.php');
7 $response->setVars(array());
8 $response->send();
9 ?>
```

At this point, we have successfully decoupled the presentation logic from the page script. We can remove the `/* PRESENTATION */` comment. It has served its purpose and is no longer needed.

However, this decoupling fundamentally breaks the presentation logic, because the view file depends on variables from the page script. With that in mind, we begin a spot check-and-modify cycle. We browse to or otherwise invoke the page script and discover that a particular variable is not available to the presentation. We add it to the setVars() array, and spot check again. We continue adding variables to the setVars() array until the view file has everything it needs, and our spot check runs become completely successful.

> For this part of the process, it would be best if we set error_reporting(E_ALL). That way we will get a PHP notice for every uninitialized variable in the presentation logic.

Given our earlier examples in *Appendix E, Code before Collecting* and *Appendix F, Code after Collecting*, we end up at *Appendix G, Code after Response View File*. We can see that the articles.html.php view file needed four variables: $id, $failure, $input, and $action:

```php
1 <?php
2 // ...
3 $response->setVars(array(
4 'id' => $id,
5 'failure' => $article_transactions->getFailure(),
6 'input' => $article_transactions->getInput(),
7 'action' => $_SERVER['PHP_SELF'],
8 ));
9 // ...
10 ?>
```

Once we have a working page script, we may wish to commit our work yet again so that we have a known correct state to which we can revert later, if needed.

Add Proper Escaping

Unfortunately, most legacy applications pay little or no attention to output security. One of the most common vulnerabilities is **cross-site scripting (XSS)**.

> **What Is XSS?**
>
> Cross-site scripting is an attack that is made possible by user input being sent back to the browser unescaped. For example, an attacker can enter maliciously-crafted JavaScript code into a form input or an HTTP header. If that value is then delivered back to the browser without being escaped, the browser will execute that JavaScript code. This has the potential to open the client browser to further attacks. For more information, please see the *OWASP entry on XSS* (`https://www.owasp.org/index.php/Cross-site_Scripting_%28XSS%29`).

The defense against XSS is to escape all variables all the time for the context in which they are used. If a variable is used as HTML content, it needs to be escaped as HTML content; if a variable is used in an HTML attribute, it needs to be escaped as such, and so on.

Defending against XSS requires diligence on the part of the developer. If we remember one thing about escaping output, it should be the `htmlspecialchars()` function. Using this function appropriately will save us from most, but not all, XSS exploits.

When using `htmlspecialchars()`, we must be sure to pass a quotes constant and a character set each time. Thus, it is not enough to call `htmlspecialchars($unescaped_text)`. We must call `htmlspecialchars($unescaped_text, ENT_QUOTES, 'UTF-8')`. So, output that looks like this:

unescaped.html.php
```
1 <form action="<?php
2 echo $request->server['PHP_SELF'];
3 ?>" method="POST">
```

This needs to be escaped like this:

escaped.html.php
```
1 <form action="<?php
2 echo htmlspecialchars(
3 $request->server['PHP_SELF'],
4 ENT_QUOTES,
5 'UTF-8'
6 );
7 ?>" method="POST">
```

Any time we send unescaped output, we need to be aware that we are likely opening up a security hole. As such, we must apply escaping to every variable we use for output.

Calling `htmlspecialchars()` repeatedly this way can be cumbersome, so the `Response` class provides an `esc()` method as an alias to `htmlspecialchars()` with reasonable settings:

escaped.php
```
1 <form action="<?php
2 echo $this->esc($request->server['PHP_SELF']);
3 ?>" method="POST">
```

Be aware that escaping via `htmlspecialchars()` is only a starting point. While escaping itself is simple to do, it can be difficult to know the appropriate escaping technique for a particular context.

Unfortunately, it is outside the scope of this book to provide a thorough overview of escaping and other security techniques. For more information, and for a good stand-alone escaping tool, please see the *Zend\Escaper* (`https://framework.zend.com/manual/2.2/en/modules/zend.escaper`) library.

After we escape all output in the `Response` view file, we can move along to testing.

Write View File Tests

Writing tests for view files presents some unique challenges. Until this chapter, all of our tests have been against classes and class methods. Because our view files are, well, *files*, we need to place them into a slightly different testing structure.

The tests/views/ directory

First, we need to create a `views/` subdirectory in our `tests/` directory. After that, our `tests/` directory should look something like this:

/path/to/app/tests/
```
1 bootstrap.php
2 classes/
3 phpunit.xml
4 views/
```

Next, we need to modify the `phpunit.xml` file so it knows to scan through the new `views/` subdirectory for tests:

tests/phpunit.xml

```
1 <phpunit bootstrap="./bootstrap.php">
2 <testsuites>
3 <testsuite>
4 <directory>./classes</directory>
5 <directory>./views</directory>
6 </testsuite>
7 </testsuites>
8 </phpunit>
```

Writing a View File Test

Now that we have a location for our view file tests, we need to write one.

Although we are testing a file, PHPUnit requires each test to be a class. As a result, we will name our test for the view file being tested, and place it in a subdirectory under `tests/views/` that mimics the original view file location. For example, if we have a view file at `views/foo/bar/baz.html.php`, we would create a test file at `tests/views/foo/bar/BazHtmlTest.php`. Yes, this is a bit ugly, but it will help us keep track of which tests map to which views.

In our test class, we will create a `Response` instance like the one at the end of our page script. We will pass into it the view file path and the needed variables. We will finally require the view, then check the output and headers to see if the view works correctly.

Given our `articles.html.php` file, our initial test might look like this:

tests/views/ArticlesHtmlTest.php

```
1 <?php
2 class ArticlesHtmlTest extends \PHPUnit_Framework_TestCase
3 {
4 protected $response;
5 protected $output;
6
7 public function setUp()
8 {
9 $this->response = new \Mlaphp\Response('/path/to/app/views');
10 $this->response->setView('articles.html.php');
11 $this->response->setVars(
12 'id' => '123',
13 'failure' => array(),
14 'action' => '/articles.php',
```

```
15 'input' => array(
16 'title' => 'Article Title',
17 'body' => 'The body text of the article.',
18 'max_ratings' => 5,
19 'credits_per_rating' => 1,
20 'notes' => '...',
21 'ready' => 0,
22 ),
23 );
24 $this->output = $this->response->requireView();
25 }
26
27 public function testBasicView()
28 {
29 $expect = '';
30 $this->assertSame($expect, $this->output);
31 }
32 }
33 ?>
```

> **Why Use requireView() Instead Of send()?**
>
> If we use `send()` the `Response` will output the view file results, instead of leaving them in a buffer for us to inspect. Calling `requireView()` invokes the view file but returns the results instead of generating output.

When we run this test, it will fail. We rejoice, because the `$expect` value is empty, but the output should have a lot of content in it. This is the correct behavior. (If the test passes, something is probably wrong.)

Asserting Correctness Of Content

Now we need our test to look at the output to see if it is correct.

The simplest way to do this is to dump the actual `$this->output` string and copy its value to the `$expect` variable. If the output string is relatively short, an `assertSame($expect, $this->output)` to make sure they are identical should be perfectly sufficient for our purposes.

However, if anything changes with any of the other files that our main view file includes, then the test will fail. The failure will occur not because the main view has changed, but because a related view has changed. That is not the kind of failure that helps us.

In the case of large output strings, we can look for an expected substring and make sure it it is present in the actual output. Then when the test fails it will be related to the particular substring for which we are testing, not to the entire output string a a whole.

For example, we can use `strpos()` to see if a particular string is in the output. If the haystack of `$this->output` does not contain the `$expect` needle, `strpos()` will return a boolean `false`. Any other value means the `$needle` is present. (This logic is easier to read if we write our own custom assertion method.)

```
1 <?php
2 public function assertOutputHas($expect)
3 {
4 if (strpos($this->output, $expect) === false) {
5 $this->fail("Did not find expected output: $expect");
6 }
7 }
8
9 public function testFormTag()
10 {
11 $expect = '<form method="POST" action="/articles.php">';
12 $this->assertOutputHas($expect);
13 }
14 ?>
```

This approach has the benefit of being very straightforward, but may not be suitable for complex assertions. We may wish to count the number of times an element occurs, or to assert that the HTML has a particular structure without referencing the contents of that structure, or to check that an element appears in the right place in the output.

For these more-complex content assertions, PHPUnit has an `assertSelectEquals()` assertion, along with other related `assertSelect*()` methods. These work by using CSS selectors to check different parts of the output, but can be difficult to read and understand.

Alternatively, we may prefer to install `Zend\Dom\Query` for finer manipulation of the DOM tree. This library also works by using CSS selectors to pick apart the content. It returns DOM nodes and node lists, which makes it very useful for testing the content in a fine-grained manner.

Unfortunately, I cannot give concrete advice on which of these approaches is best for you. I suggest starting with an approach similar to the `assertOutputHas()` method above, and moving along to the `Zend\Dom\Query` approach when it becomes obvious that you need a more powerful system.

After we have written tests that confirm the presentation works as it should, we move on to the last part of the process.

Commit, Push, Notify QA

At this point we should have passing tests for the page script and for the extracted presentation logic. We now commit all our code and tests, push them to the common repository, and notify QA that we are ready for them to look over the new work.

Do ... While

We continue to search for presentation logic mixed in with business logic in our page scripts. When we have extracted all presentation logic to view files via `Response` objects, we are done.

Common Questions

What about Headers and Cookies?

In the above examples we paid attention only to output from `echo` and `print`. However, it is often the case that a page script will also set HTTP headers via `header()`, `setcookie()`, and `setrawcookie()`. These, too, generate output.

Dealing with these output methods can be problematic. Whereas the `Response` class uses `output buffering` to capture `echo` and `print` into return values, there is no similar option for buffering calls to `header()` and related functions. Because the output from these functions is not buffered, we cannot easily test to see what's going on.

This is one place where having a `Response` object really helps us. The class comes with methods that buffer the `header()` and related native PHP functions, but do not call those functions until `send()` time. This allows us to capture the inputs to these calls and test them before they are actually activated.

For example, say we have some code like this in a contrived view file:

foo.json.php
```
1  <?php
2  header('Content-Type: application/json');
3  setcookie('baz', 'dib');
4  setrawcookie('zim', 'gir');
5  echo json_encode($data);
6  ?>
```

Among other things, we cannot test that the headers are what we expect them to be. PHP has already sent them to the client.

When using a view file with a *Response* object, we can prefix the native function calls with $this-> to call a *Response* method instead of the native PHP function. The *Response* methods buffer the arguments to the native calls instead of making the calls directly. This allows us to inspect the arguments before they are delivered as output.

foo.json.php

```
1 <?php
2 $this->header('Content-Type: application/json');
3 $this->setcookie('baz', 'dib');
4 $this->setrawcookie('zim', 'gir');
5 echo json_encode($data);
6 ?>
```

> Because the view file is being executed inside the *Response* instance, it has access to $this for the Response properties and methods. The header(), setcookie(), and setrawcookie() methods on the Response object have the exact same signatures as the native PHP methods, but capture the inputs into a property for later output instead of generating output immediately.

We can now test the Response object to check the HTTP body as well as the HTTP headers.

tests/views/FooJsonTest.php

```
1 <?php
2 public function test()
3 {
4 // set up the response object
5 $response = new \Mlaphp\Response('/path/to/app/views');
6 $response->setView('foo.json.php');
7 $response->setVars('data', array('foo' => 'bar'));
8
9 // invoke the view file and test its output
10 $expect_body = '{"foo":"bar"}';
11 $actual_body = $response->requireView();
12 $this->assertSame($expect_output, $actual_output);
13
14 // test the buffered HTTP header calls
15 $expect_headers = array(
16 array('header', 'Content-Type: application/json'),
17 array('setcookie', 'baz', 'dib'),
```

```
18 array('setrawcookie', 'zim', 'gir'),
19 );
20 $actual_headers = $response->getHeaders();
21 $this->assertSame($expect_output, $actual_output);
22 }
23 ?>
```

> The *Response* getHeaders() method returns an array of sub-arrays.
> Each sub-array has an element 0 indicating the native PHP function name
> to be called, and the remaining elements are arguments to the function.
> These are the function calls that will be made at send() time.

What if we already have a Template system?

Many times, a legacy application will have a view or template system already in place. If so, it may be sufficient to keep using the existing template system instead of introducing a new Response class.

If we decide to keep an existing template system, the other steps in this chapter still apply. We need to move all of the template calls to a single location at the end of the page script, disentangling all of the template interactions from the rest of the business logic. We can then display the template at the end of the page script. For example:

foo.php
```
1 <?php
2 // ... business logic ...
3
4 /* PRESENTATION */
5 $template = new Template;
6 $template->assign($this->getVars());
7 $template->display('foo.tpl.php');
8 ?>
```

If we are not sending HTTP headers, this approach is just as testable as using a Response object. However, if we mix in calls to header() and related functions, our testability will be more limited.

In the interest of future-proofing our legacy code, we may move the template logic to a view file, and interact with a `Response` object in our page script instead. For example:

foo.php
```php
1 <?php
2 // ... business logic ...
3
4 /* PRESENTATION */
5 $response = new Response('/path/to/app/views');
6 $response->setView('foo.html.php');
7 $response->setVars(array('foo' => $foo));
8 $response->send();
9 ?>
```

foo.html.php
```php
1 <?php
2 // buffer calls to HTTP headers
3 $this->setcookie('foo', 'bar');
4 $this->setrawcookie('baz', 'dib');
5
6 // set up the template object with Response vars
7 $template = new Template;
8 $template->assign($this->getVars());
9
10 // display the template
11 $template->display('foo.tpl.php');
12 ?>
```

This allows us to keep using the existing template logic and files, while adding testability for HTTP headers via the `Response` object.

For consistency's sake, we should either use the existing template system or wrap all template logic in view files via `Response` objects. We should not use the template system in some page scripts and the `Response` object in others. In later chapters, it will be important that we have a single way of interacting with the presentation layer in our page scripts.

What about Streaming Content?

Most of the time, our presentation is small enough that it can be buffered into memory by PHP until it is ready to send. However, sometimes our legacy application may need to send large amounts of data, such as a file that is tens or hundreds of megabytes.

Reading a large file into memory so that we can output it to the user is usually not a good approach. Instead, we stream the file: we read a small piece of the file and send it to the user, then read the next small piece and send it to the user, and so on until the whole file has been delivered. That way, we never have to keep the entire file in memory.

The examples so far have only dealt with buffering a view into memory and then outputting it all at once, not with streaming. It would be a poor approach for our view file to read the entire resource into memory and then output it. At the same time, we need to make sure headers are delivered before any streamed content.

The Response object has a method to handle this situation. The Response method setLastCall() allows us to set a user-defined function (a callable) to invoke after requiring the view file and sending the headers. With this, we can pass a class method that will stream the resource out for us.

For example, say we need to stream out a large image file. We can write a class like the following to handle the stream logic:

classes/FileStreamer.php
```php
1 <?php
2 class FileStreamer
3 {
4 public function send($file, $dest = STDOUT)
5 {
6 $fh = fopen($file, 'rb');
7 while (! feof($fh)) {
8 $data = fread($fh, 8192);
9 fwrite($dest, $data);
10 }
11 fclose($fh);
12 }
13 }
14 ?>
```

There is much to be desired here, such as error checking and better resource handling, but it accomplishes the purpose for our example.

We can then create an instance of the *FileStreamer* in our page script, and the view file can use it as the callable argument for setLastCall():

foo.php
```php
1 <?php
2 // ... business logic ...
3 $file_streamer = new FileStreamer;
```

```
4 $image_file = '/path/to/picture.tiff';
5 $content_type = 'image/tiff';
6
7 /* PRESENTATION */
8 $response = new Response('/path/to/app/views');
9 $response->setView('foo.stream.php');
10 $response->setVars(array(
11 'streamer' => $file_streamer,
12 'file' => $image_file,
13 'type' => $content_type,
14 ));
15 ?>
```

views/foo.stream.php
```
1 <?php
2 $this->header("Content-Type: {$type}");
3 $this->setLastCall(array($streamer, 'send'), $file);
4 ?>
```

At `send()` time, the `Response` will require the view file, which sets a header and the last call with arguments. The `Response` then sends the headers and the captured output of the view (which in this case is nothing). Finally, it invokes the callable and arguments from `setLastCall()`, which streams out the file.

What if we have lots of Presentation variables?

In the example code from this chapter, we had only a handful of variables to pass to the presentation logic. Unfortunately, it is more likely that there will be 10 or 20 or more variables to pass. This is usually because the presentation is composed of several `include` files, each of which needs its own variables.

These extra variables are usually needed for things like the site header, navigation, and footer portions. Because we have decoupled the business logic from the presentation logic and are executing the presentation logic in a separate scope, we have to pass in all the variables needed for all the `include` files.

Say we have a view file that includes a `header.php` file, like this:

header.php
```
1 <html>
2 <head>
3 <title><?php
4 echo $this->esc($page_title);
```

```
5 ?></title>
6 <link rel="stylesheet" href="<?php
7 echo $this->esc($page_style);
8 ?>"></link>
9 </head>
10 <body>
11 <h1><?php echo $this->esc($page_title); ?></h1>
12 <div id="navigation">
13 <ul>
14 <?php foreach ($site_nav as $nav_item) {
Extract Presentation Logic To View Files 117
15 $href = $this->esc($nav_item['href']);
16 $name = $this->esc($nav_item['name']);
17 echo '<li><a href="' . $href
18 . '"/a>' . $name
19 . '</li>' . PHP_EOL;
20 }?>
21 </ul>
22 </div>
23 <!-- end of header.php -->
```

Our page script will have to pass `$page_title`, `$page_style`, and `$site_nav` variables in order for the header to display properly. This is a relatively tame case; there could be many more variables than this.

One solution is to collect commonly-used variables into one or more objects of their own. We can then pass those common-use objects into the _Response_ for the view file to use. For example, header-specific display variables can be placed in a `HeaderDisplay` class, which can then be passed to the _Response_.

```
classes/HeaderDisplay.php
1 <?php
2 class HeaderDisplay
3 {
4 public $page_title;
5 public $page_style;
6 public $site_nav;
7 }
8 ?>
```

We can then modify the `header.php` file to use the *HeaderDisplay* object, and the page script can pass an instance of *HeaderDisplay* instead of all the separate header-related variables.

> Once we begin collecting related variables into classes, we will begin to see how we can collect presentation logic into methods on those classes, and thereby reduce the amount of logic in our view files. For example, it should not be hard for us to imagine a `getNav()` method on the *HeaderDisplay* class that returns the proper HTML for our navigation widgets.

What about class methods that generate output?

In the example code for this chapter, we concentrated on presentation logic in page scripts. However, it may be the case that domain classes or other support classes use `echo` or `header()` to generate output. Because output generation must be restricted to the presentation layer, we need to find a way to remove these calls without breaking our legacy application. Even classes that are intended for presentation purposes should not generate output on their own.

The solution here is to convert each use of `echo`, `print`, and so on to a `return`. We can then either output the result immediately, or capture the result into a variable and output it later.

For example, say we have a class method that looks like this:

```
1 <?php
2 public function namesAndRoles($list)
3 {
4 echo "<p>Names and roles:</p>";
5 foreach ($list as $item) {
6 echo "<dl>";
7 echo "<dt>Name</dt><dd>{$item['name']}</dd>";
8 echo "<dt>Role</dt><dd>{$item['role']}</dd>";
9 echo "</dl>";
10 }
11 }
12 ?>
```

We can convert it to something like this instead (and remember to add escaping!):

```
1 <?php
2 public function namesAndRoles($list)
3 {
4 $html = "<p>Names and roles:</p>";
5 foreach ($list as $item) {
6 $name = htmlspecialchars($item['name'], ENT_QUOTES, 'UTF-8');
7 $role = htmlspecialchars($item['role'], ENT_QUOTES, 'UTF-8');
```

```
 8 $html .= "<dl>";
 9 $html .= "<dt>Name</dt><dd>{$name}</dd>";
10 $html .= "<dt>Role</dt><dd>{$role}</dd>";
11 $html .= "</dl>";
12 }
13 return $html;
14 }
15 ?>
```

What about Business Logic Mixed into the presentation?

When rearranging the page script to separate the business logic from the presentation logic, we may discover that the presentation code makes calls to *Transactions* or other classes or resources. This is a pernicious form of mixing concerns, since the presentation is dependent on the results of these calls.

If the called code is specifically for output, then there's no problem; we can leave the calls in place. But if the called code interacts with an external resource such as a database or a network connection, we have a mixing of concerns that needs to be separated.

The solution is to extract an equivalent set of business logic calls from the presentation logic, capture the results to a variable, and then pass that variable to the presentation.

For a contrived example, the following mixed code makes database calls and then presents them in a single loop:

```
1 <?php
2 /* PRESENTATION */
3 foreach ($post_transactions->fetchTopTenPosts() as $post) {
4 echo "{$post['title']} has "
5 . $comment_transactions->fetchCountForPost($post['id'])
6 . " comments.";
7 }
8 ?>
```

Ignore for a moment that we need to solve the N+1 query problem presented in the example, and that this might better be solved at the *Transactions* level. How can we disentangle the presentation from the data retrieval?

In this case, we build an equivalent set of code to capture the needed data, then pass that data to the presentation logic, and apply proper escaping:

```
1 <?php
2 // ...
3 $posts = $post_transactions->fetchTopTenPosts();
4 foreach ($posts as &$post) {
5 $count = $comment_transactions->fetchCountForPost($post['id']);
6 $post['comment_count'] = $count;
7 }
8 // ...
9
10 /* PRESENTATION */
11 foreach ($posts as $post) {
12 $title = $this->esc($post['title']);
13 $comment_count = $this->esc($post['comment_count']);
14 echo "{$title} has {$comment_count} comments."
15 }
16 ?>
```

Yes, we end up looping over the same data twice -- once in the business logic, and once in the presentation logic. While this may reasonably be called inefficient in some ways, efficiency is not our primary goal. Separation of concerns is our primary goal, and this approach achieves that nicely.

What if a page contains only presentation logic?

Some of the pages in our legacy application may consist mostly or entirely of presentation code. In these cases, it may seem like we don't need a *Response* object.

However, even these page scripts should be converted to use a *Response* and a view file. A later step in our modernization process is going to require a consistent interface to the results of our page scripts, and our *Response* object is the way to ensure that consistency.

Review and next steps

We have now gone through all of our page scripts and extracted the presentation logic to a series of separate files. The presentation code is now executed in a scope competely independent from the page script. This makes it very easy for us to see the remaining logic of the script, as well as test the presentation logic independently.

With the presentation logic extracted to its own layer, our page scripts are dwindling in size. All that remains in them is some setup work and the action logic needed to prepare a response.

Our next step, then, is to extract the remaining action logic from our page scripts to a series of controller classes.

11
Extract Action Logic to Controllers

Thus far, we have extracted our model domain logic and our view presentation logic. Only two kinds of logic remain in our page scripts:

- Dependency logic, which uses the application settings to create objects
- Action logic (sometimes called business logic) which uses those objects to perform the page actions

In this chapter, we will extract a layer of `Controller` classes from our page scripts. These will handle the remaining action logic in our legacy application separately from our dependency-creation logic.

Embedded action logic

For an example of embedded action logic mixed with dependency logic, we can look at the ending example code from the last chapter in *Appendix G, Code after Response View File*. Therein, we do a little setup work, then we check some conditions and call different parts of our domain `Transactions`, and at the end we put together a `Response` object to send our response to the client.

As was the problem with mixed-in presentation logic, we cannot test the action logic separately from rest of the page script. Similarly, we cannot easily change the dependency creation logic to make the page script more testable.

We solve the problem of embedded action logic as we did with embedded presentation logic. We must extract the action code to a class of its own to separate the various remaining concerns of our page script. This will also allow us to test the action logic independently from the rest of the application.

The Extraction Process

Extracting the action logic from our page scripts should be a relatively easy task for us now. Because the domain layer has been extracted, along with the presentation layer, the action logic should be obvious. The work itself still rewards attention to detail, in that the main issue will be picking apart the dependency setup portions from the action logic itself.

In general, the process is as follows:

1. Find a page script where action logic is still mixed in with the rest of the code.

2. In that page script, rearrange the code so that all action logic is in its own central block. Spot check the rearranged code to make sure it still works properly.

3. Extract the central block of action logic to a new `Controller` class, and modify the page script to use the new `Controller`. Spot check the page script with the *Controller* in place.

4. Write a unit test for the new `Controller` class and spot check again.

5. Commit the new code and tests, push them to the common repository, and notify QA.

6. Find another page script with embedded action logic and start again; when all page scripts use `Controller` objects, we are done.

Search for Embedded Action Logic

At this point, we should be able to find action logic without having to use our project-wide search facility. Every page script in our legacy application probably has at least a little bit of action logic left in it.

Rearrange the Page Script and Spot Check

When we have a candidate page script, we proceed to rearrange the code so that all setup and dependency-creation work is at the top, all the action logic is in the middle, and the `$response->send()` call is at the bottom. For our starting example here, we will use the code from the end of the last chapter as found in *Appendix G, Code after Response View File*.

Identify Code Blocks

First, we go to the very top of the script and place a /* DEPENDENCY */ comment on the first line (or perhaps after the inclusion of a setup script). Then we go to the very end of the script, to the $response->send() line, and place a /* FINISHED */ comment above it.

Now we reach a point where we must use our professional judgment. On some line after the setup and dependency work in the page script, we will see that the code begins to perform some sort of action logic. Our assessment of just where this transition occurs may be somewhat arbitrary, since the action logic and setup logic are likely to still be intertwined. Even so, we must pick a point at which we believe the action logic really gets started, and place a /* CONTROLLER */ comment there.

Move Code to Its Related Block

Once we have identified these three blocks in the page script, we begin rearranging the code so that only setup and dependency-creation work occurs between /* DEPENDENCY */ and /* CONTROLLER */, and only action logic occurs between /* CONTROLLER */ and /* FINISHED */.

In general, we should avoid conditions or loops in the dependency block, and avoid object creation in the controller block. The code in the dependency block should only create objects, and the code in the controller block should only operate on objects that have been created in the dependency block.

Given our starting code in *Appendix G, Code after Response View File*, we can see the result of an example rearrangement in *Appendix H, Code after Controller Rearrangement*. Of note, we moved the $user_id declaration down to the controller block, and we moved the Response object creation up to the dependency block. The original action logic in the central controller block remains otherwise unchanged.

Spot Check the Rearranged Code

Finally, after rearranging the page script, we need to spot check our changes to make sure everything still works properly. If we have characterization tests, we should run those. Otherwise, we should browse to or otherwise invoke the page script. If it does not work correctly, we need to undo and redo our rearrangement so that we fix whatever errors we have introduced.

When our spot check runs are successful, we may wish to commit our changes so far. This will give us a known-working state to which we can revert if future changes go bad.

Extract a Controller Class

Now that we have a rearranged page script that works properly, we can extract the central controller block to a class of its own. This is not difficult, but we will do it in several sub-steps to make sure everything goes smoothly.

Pick a Class Name

Before we can extract to a class, we need to pick a name for the class we will extract to.

With our domain-layer classes, we chose the top-level namespace *Domain*. Because this is a controller layer, we will use the top-level namespace *Controller*. The namespace we use is not as important as consistently using the same namespace for all controllers. Personally, I prefer *Controller* because it is broad enough to encompass different kinds of controllers, such as Application Controller.

The class name within that namespace should reflect where the page script is in the URL hierarchy, with namespace separators where there are directory separators in the path. This approach makes it obvious what the original page script directory path was, and keeps the subdirectories organized nicely in the class structure. We also suffix the class name with `Page` to indicate it is a Page Controller.

For example, if the page script is at `/foo/bar/baz.php`, the class name should be `Controller\Foo\Bar\BazPage`. The class file itself would then be placed in our central classes directory under `classes/Controller/Foo/Bar/BazPage.php`.

Create a Skeleton Class File

Once we have a class name, we can create a skeleton class file for it. We add two empty methods as placeholders for later: the `__invoke()` method will receive the action logic from the page script, and the constructor will eventually receive dependencies for the class.

```
classes/Controller/Foo/Bar/BazPage.php
1 <?php
2 namespace Controller\Foo\Bar;
3
4 class BazPage
5 {
6 public function __construct()
7 {
8 }
9
```

```
10 public function __invoke()
11 {
12 }
13 }
14 ?>
```

Why __invoke()?

Personally, I enjoy co-opting the __invoke() magic method for this purpose, but you may wish to use exec() or some other appropriate term to indicate we are executing or otherwise running the controller. Whatever method name we choose, we should use it consistently.

Move the Action Logic and Spot Check

Now we are ready to extract the action logic to our new Controller class.

First, we cut the controller block from the page script, and paste it into the __invoke() method as-is. We add one line to the end of the action logic, return $response, to send the *Response* object back to the calling code.

Next, we go back to the page script. In the place of the extracted action logic, we create an instance of our new Controller and call its __invoke() method, getting back a *Response* object.

We should always use the same variable name for the *Controller* object in all of our page scripts. All the examples here will use the name $controller. This is not because the name $controller is special, but because this level of consistency will be very important in a later chapter.

At this point, we have successfully decoupled the action logic from the page script. However, this decoupling fundamentally breaks the action logic, because the *Controller* depends on variables from the page script.

With that in mind, we begin a spot-check-and-modify cycle. We browse to or otherwise invoke the page script and discover that a particular variable is not available to the *Controller*. We add it to the __invoke() method signature, and spot check again. We continue adding variables to the __invoke() method until the *Controller* has everything it needs and our spot check runs become completely successful.

> For this part of the process, it would be best if we set `error_reporting(E_ALL)`. That way we will get a PHP notice for every uninitialized variable in the action logic.

Given our rearranged page script in *Appendix H, Code after Controller Rearrangement*, the result of our initial extraction to a *Controller* can be seen in *Appendix I, Code after Controller Extraction*. It turns out that the extracted action logic needed four variables: `$request`, `$response`, `$user`, and `$article_transactions`.

Convert Controller to Dependency Injection and Spot Check

Once we have a working block of action logic in the `__invoke()` method, we will convert the method parameters into constructor parameters so that the *Controller* can use dependency injection.

First, we cut the `__invoke()` parameters and paste them as a whole into the `__construct()` parameters. We then edit the class definition and `__construct()` method to retain the parameters as properties.

Next, we modify the `__invoke()` method to use the class properties instead of the method parameters. That means prefixing each of the needed variables with `$this->`.

Then, we go back to the page script. We cut the arguments to the `__invoke()` call, and paste them into the *Controller* instantiation.

Now that we have converted the *Controller* to dependency injection, we need to spot check the page script again to make sure everything works properly. If it does not, we need to undo and redo our conversion until our tests pass.

At this point, we can remove the `/* DEPENDENCY */`, `/* CONTROLLER */`, and `/* FINISHED */` comments. They have served their purpose and are no longer needed.

Given the `__invoke()` usage in *Appendix I, Code after Controller Extraction*, we can see what converting the *Controller* to dependency injection looks like in *Appendix J, Code after Controller Dependency Injection*. We have moved the *Controller* `__invoke()` parameters up to `__construct()`, retained them as properties, used the new properties in the `__invoke()` method body, and modified the page script to pass the needed variables at `new` time instead of `__invoke()` time.

Once we have a working page script, we may wish to commit our work yet again so that we have a known correct state to which we can revert later, if needed.

Write a Controller Test

Even though we have tested our page script, we need to write a unit test for our extracted *Controller* logic. When we write the test, we will need to inject all the needed dependencies into our *Controller*, preferably as test doubles like fakes or mocks so we can isolate the *Controller* from the rest of the system.

When we make assertions, they should probably be against the *Response* object returned from the `__invoke()` method. We can use `getView()` to make sure the right view file is set, `getVars()` to inspect the variables to be used in the view, and `getLastCall()` to see if the final callable (if any) has been set properly.

Commit, Push, Notify QA

Once we have a passing unit test, and our tests of the original page script also pass, we can commit our new code and tests. Then we push to the common repository and notify QA that we are ready for them to review our work.

Do ... While

Now we go on to the next page script that has embedded action logic and begin the extraction process over again. When all of our page scripts use dependency-injected *Controller* objects, we are done.

Common Questions

Can we pass parameters to the Controller method?

In the examples, we remove all parameters from the `__invoke()` method. However, sometimes we will want to pass a parameter to that method as last-minute information for the controller logic.

In general, we should avoid doing so at this point in our modernization process. This is not because it is a poor practice, but because we need a very high level of consistency in our controller invocations for a later modernization step. The most-consistent thing is for there to be no `__invoke()` parameters at all.

If we need to pass extra information to the *Controller*, we should do so via the constructor. This is especially the case when we are passing request values.

For example, instead of this:

page_script.php

```php
1 <?php
2 /* DEPENDENCY */
3 // ...
4 $response = new \Mlaphp\Response('/path/to/app/views');
5 $foo_transactions = new \Domain\Foo\FooTransactions(...);
6 $controller = new \Controller\Foo(
7 $response,
8 $foo_transactions
9 );
10
11 /* CONTROLLER */
12 $response = $controller->__invoke('update', $_POST['user_id']);
13
14 /* FINISHED */
15 $response->send();
16 ?>
```

We could do this:

page_script.php

```php
1 <?php
2 /* DEPENDENCY */
3 // ...
4 $response = new \Mlaphp\Response('/path/to/app/views');
5 $foo_transactions = new \Domain\Foo\FooTransactions(...);
6 $request = new \Mlaphp\Request($GLOBALS);
7 $controller = new \Controller\Foo(
8 $response,
9 $foo_transactions,
10 $request
11 );
12
13 /* CONTROLLER */
14 $response = $controller->__invoke();
15
16 /* FINISHED */
17 $response->send();
18 ?>
```

The __invoke() method body would then use $this->request->get['item_id'].

Can a Controller have Multiple actions?

In the examples, our *Controller* objects perform a single action. However, it is often the case that a page controller encompasses multiple actions, such as both inserting and updating a database record.

Our first pass at extracting action logic from the page script should keep the code pretty much intact, making allowances for properties instead of local variables and so on. Once the code is in the class, though, it is perfectly reasonable to split the logic into separate action methods. Then the __invoke() method can become little more than a `switch` statement that picks the correct action method. If we do so, we should be sure to update our *Controller* tests, and continue to spot check the page script to make sure our changes do not break anything.

Note that if we create additional *Controller* action methods, we need to avoid calling them from our page script. For the sake of the consistency needed in a later modernization step, the __invoke() method should be the only *Controller* method our page script calls in its controller block.

What If the Controller contains include Calls?

Unfortunately, as we go about rearranging a page script, we are likely to discover that we still have several `include` calls in the controller block. (Calls to `include` for setup and dependency purposes are not such a big deal, especially if they are the same in every page script.)

Having `include` calls in the controller block is an artifact of the include-oriented architecture with which our legacy application began. It is a particularly difficult problem to solve. We want to encapsulate action logic in classes, not in files that execute behavior the moment we `include` them.

For now, we must submit ourselves to the idea that `include` calls in the controller block of our page scripts are ugly but necessary. We should avert our eyes if needed and copy them into the `Controller` class with the rest of the controller code from the page script.

As consolation, we will solve the problem of these embedded `include` calls in the next chapter.

Review and next steps

The extraction of the action logic to a layer of *Controllers* completes a huge modernization goal for our legacy application. We now have a full Model View Controller system in place: a domain layer for models, a presentation layer for views, and a controller layer that connects the two.

We should feel very satisfied about our modernization progress. The code that remains in each page script is a shadow of its original self. Most of the logic is wiring code that creates a *Controller* with its dependencies. The remaining logic is the same across all page scripts; it invokes the *Controller* and sends the returned *Response* object.

However, there is a major legacy artifact for us to deal with. To finish a full extraction and encapsulation of controller logic, we need to remove any remaining `include` calls embedded in our *Controller* classes.

12
Replace Includes in Classes

Even though we have Model View Controller separation now, we may still have many include calls in our classes. We want our legacy application to be free from the artifacts of its include-oriented heritage, where merely including a file causes logic to be executed. To do so, we will need to replace include calls with method calls throughout our classes.

[For the purposes of this chapter, we will use the term include to cover not just include but also require, include_once, and require_once.]

Embedded include Calls

Let's say we extracted some action logic with an embedded include to a *Controller* method. The code receives information on a new user, calls an include to perform some common validation functionality, and then deals with success or failure of validation:

classes/Controller/NewUserPage.php
```php
1 <?php
2 public function __invoke()
3 {
4 // ...
5 $user = $this->request->post['user'];
6 include 'includes/validators/validate_new_user.php';
7 if ($user_is_valid) {
8 $this->user_transactions->addNewUser($user);
9 $this->response->setVars('success' => true);
10 } else {
11 $this->response->setVars(array(
12 'success' => false,
```

```
13 'user_messages' => $user_messages
14 ));
15 }
16
17 return $this->response;
18 }
19 ?>
```

Here is an example of what the included file might look like:

```
includes/validators/validate_new_user.php
1 <?php
2 $user_messages = array();
3 $user_is_valid = true;
4
5 if (! Validate::email($user['email'])) {
6 $user_messages[] = 'Email is not valid.';
7 $user_is_valid = false;
8 }
9
10 if (! Validate::strlen($foo['username'], 6, 8)) {
11 $user_messages[] = 'Username must be 6-8 characters long.';
12 $user_is_valid = false;
13 }
14
15 if ($user['password'] !== $user['confirm_password']) {
16 $user_messages[] = 'Passwords do not match.';
17 $user_is_valid = false;
18 }
19 ?>
```

Let us ignore for now the specifics of the validation code. The point here is that the `include` file and any code using it are both tightly coupled to each other. Any code using the file has to initialize a `$user` variable before including it. Any code using the file also has an expectation of getting two new variables introduced into its scope (`$user_messages` and `$user_is_valid`).

We want to decouple this logic so that the logic in the `include` file does not intrude on the scope of the class methods in which is it used. We do this by extracting the logic of the `include` file to a class of its own.

The Replacement process

The difficulty of extracting includes to their own classes depends on the number and complexity of the `include` calls remaining in our class files. If there are very few includes and they are relatively simple, the process will be easy to complete. If there are many complex interdependent includes, the process will be relatively difficult to work through.

In general, the process is as follows:

1. Search the `classes/` directory for an `include` call in a class.
2. For that `include` call, search the entire codebase to find how many times the included file is used.
3. If the included file is used only once, and only in that one class:
    1. Copy the contents of the included file code as-is directly over the `include` call.
    2. Test the modified class, and delete the include file.
    3. Refactor the copied code so that it follows all our existing rules: no globals, no `new`, inject dependencies, return instead of output, and no `include` calls.
4. If the included file is used more than once:
    1. Copy the contents of the included file as-is to a new class method.
    2. Replace the discovered `include` call with inline instantiation of the new class and invocation of the new method.
    3. Test the class in which the `include` was replaced to find coupled variables; add these to the new method signature by reference.
    4. Search the entire codebase for `include` calls to that same file, and replace each with inline instantiation and invocation; spot check modified files and test modified classes.
    5. Delete the original `include` file; unit test and spot check the entire legacy application.
    6. Write a unit test for the new class, and refactor the new class so that it follows all our existing rules: no globals, no superglobals, no `new`, inject dependencies, return-not-output, and no includes.
    7. Finally, replace each inline instantiation of the new class in each of our class files with dependency injection, testing along the way.

5. Commit, push, notify QA.

6. Repeat until there are no `include` calls in any of our classes.

Search for include Calls

First, as we did in a much earlier chapter, we use our project-wide search facility to find `include` calls. In this case, search only the `classes/` directory with the following regular expression:

```
^[ \t]*(include|include_once|require|require_once)
```

This should give us a list of candidate `include` calls in the `classes/` directory.

We pick a single `include` file to work with, then search the entire codebase for other inclusions of the same file. For example, if we found this candidate `include` ...

```
1 <?php
2 require 'foo/bar/baz.php';
3 ?>
```

We would search the entire codebase for `include` calls to the file name `baz.php`:

```
^[ \t]*(include|include_once|require|require_once).*baz\.php
```

We search only for the file name because, depending on where the `include` call is located, the relative directory paths might lead to the same file. It is up to us to determine which of these `include` calls reference the same file.

Once we have a list of `include` calls that we know lead to the same file, we count the number of calls that include that file. If there is only one call, our work is relatively simple. If there is more than one call, our work is more complex.

Replacing a Single include Call

If a file is used as the target of an `include` call only once, it is relatively easy to remove the `include`.

First, we copy the entire contents of the `include` file. We move back to the class where the `include` occurs, delete the `include` call, and paste the entire contents of the `include` file in its place.

Next, we run the unit tests for the class to make sure it still works properly. If they fail, we rejoice! We have found errors to be corrected before we continue. If they pass, we likewise rejoice, and move on.

Now that the `include` call has been replaced, and the file contents have been successfully transplanted to the class, we delete the include file. It is no longer needed.

Finally, we can return to our class file where the newly transplanted code lives. We refactor it according to all the rules we have learned so far: no globals or superglobals, no use of the `new` keyword outside of factories, inject all needed dependencies, return values instead of generating output, and (recursively) no `include` calls. We run our unit tests along the way to make sure we do not break any pre-existing functionality.

Replacing Multiple include Calls

If a file is used as the target of multiple `include` calls, it will take more work to replace them.

Copy include file to Class Method

First, we will copy the `include` code to a class method of its own. To do this, we need to pick a class name appropriate to the purpose of the included file. Alternatively, we may name the class based on the path to the included file so we can keep track of where the code came from originally.

As for the method name, we again pick something appropriate to the purpose of the `include` code. Personally, if the class is going to contain only a single method, I like to co-opt the `__invoke()` method for this. However, if there end up being multiple methods, we need to pick a sensible name for each one.

Once we have picked a class name and method, we create the new class in the proper file location, and copy the `include` code directly into the new method. (We do not delete the include file itself just yet.)

Replace the original include Call

Now that we have a class to work with, we go back to the `include` call we discovered in our search, replace it with an inline instantiation of the new class, and invoke the new method.

For example, say the original calling code looked like this:

```
Calling Code
1 <?php
2 // ...
3 include 'includes/validators/validate_new_user.php';
4 // ...
5 ?>
```

If we extracted the include code to a Validator\NewUserValidator class as its __
invoke() method body, we might replace the include call with this:

Calling Code
```
1 <?php
2 // ...
3 $validator = new \Validator\NewUserValidator;
4 $validator->__invoke();
5 // ...
6 ?>
```

> Using inline instantiation in a class violates one of our rules regarding
> dependency injection. We do not want to use the new keyword outside
> of factory classes. We do so here only to facilitate the refactoring process.
> Later, we will replace this inline instantiation with injection.

Discover coupled variables through testing

We have now successfully decoupled the calling code from the include file, but this
leaves us with a problem. Because the calling code executed the include code inline,
the variables needed by the newly-extracted code are no longer available. We need to
pass into the new class method all the variables it needs for execution, and to make
its variables available to the calling code when the method is done.

To do so, we run the unit tests for the class that called the include. The tests will
reveal to us what variables are needed by the new method. We can then pass these
into the method by reference. Using a reference makes sure that both blocks of code
are operating on the exact same variables, just as if the include was still being
executed inline. This minimizes the number of changes we need to make to the
calling code and the newly extracted code.

For example, say we have extracted the code from an include file to this class
and method:

classes/Validator/NewUserValidator.php
```
1 <?php
2 namespace Validator;
3
4 class NewUserValidator
5 {
6 public function __invoke()
7 {
8 $user_messages = array();
```

```
 9 $user_is_valid = true;
10
11 if (! Validate::email($user['email'])) {
12 $user_messages[] = 'Email is not valid.';
13 $user_is_valid = false;
14 }
15
16 if (! Validate::strlen($foo['username'], 6, 8)) {
17 $user_messages[] = 'Username must be 6-8 characters long.';
18 $user_is_valid = false;
19 }
20
21 if ($user['password'] !== $user['confirm_password']) {
22 $user_messages[] = 'Passwords do not match.';
23 $user_is_valid = false;
24 }
25 }
26 }
27 ?>
```

When we test the class that calls this code in place of an include, the tests will
fail, because the $user value is not available to the new method, and the $user_
messages and $user_is_valid variables are not available to the calling code.
We rejoice at the failure, because it tells us what we need to do next! We add each
missing variable to the method signature by reference:

classes/Validator/NewUserValidator.php
```
1 <?php
2 public function __invoke(&$user, &$user_messages, &$user_is_valid)
3 ?>
```

We then pass the variables to the method from the calling code:

classes/Validator/NewUserValidator.php
```
1 <?php
2 $validator->__invoke($user, $user_messages, $user_is_valid);
3 ?>
```

We continue running the unit tests until they all pass, adding variables as needed.
When all the tests pass, we rejoice! All the needed variables are now available in both
scopes, and the code itself will remain decoupled and testable.

> Not all variables in the extracted code may be needed by the calling code, and vice versa. We should let the unit testing failures guide us as to which variables need to be passed in as references.

Replace other include Calls and Test

Now that we have decoupled our original calling code from the `include` file, we need to decouple all other remaining code from the same file. Given our earlier search results, we go to each file and replace the relevant `include` call with an inline instantiation of the new class. We then add a line that calls the new method with the needed variables.

Note that we may be replacing code within classes, or within non-class files such as view files. If we replace code in a class, we should run the unit tests for that class to make sure the replacement does not break anything. If we replace code in a non-class file, we should run the test for that file if it exists (such as a view file test), or else spot check the file if no tests exist for it.

Delete the include file and test

Once we have replaced all `include` calls to the file, we delete the file. We should now run all of our tests and spot checks for the entire legacy application to make sure that we did not miss an `include` call to that file. If a test or spot check fails, we need to remedy it before continuing.

Write a test and refactor

Now that the legacy application works just as it used to before we extracted the `include` code to its own class, we write a unit test for the new class.

Once we have a passing unit test for the new class, we refactor the code in that class according to all the rules we have learned so far: no globals or superglobals, no use of the `new` keyword outside of factories, inject all needed dependencies, return values instead of generating output, and (recursively) no `include` calls. We continue to run our tests along the way to make sure we do not break any pre-existing functionality.

Convert to Dependency Injection and test

When the unit test for our newly refactored class passes, we proceed to replace all our inline instantiations with dependency injection. We do so only in our class files; in our view files and other non-class files, the inline instantiation is not much of a problem

For example, we may see this inline instantiation and invocation in a class:

classes/Controller/NewUserPage.php

```php
1  <?php
2  namespace Controller;
3
4  class NewUserPage
5  {
6  // ...
7
8  public function __invoke()
9  {
10 // ...
11 $user = $this->request->post['user'];
12
13 $validator = new \Validator\NewUserValidator;
14 $validator->__invoke($user, $user_messages, $u
15
16 if ($user_is_valid) {
17 $this->user_transactions->addNewUser($user
18 $this->response->setVars('success' => true
19 } else {
20 $this->response->setVars(array(
21 'success' => false,
22 'user_messages' => $user_messages
23 ));
24 }
25
26 return $this->response;
27 }
28 }
29 ?>
```

We move the `$validator` to a property injected via the constructor, and use the property in the method:

classes/Controller/NewUserPage.php

```php
1  <?php
2  namespace Controller;
3
4  class NewUserPage
5  {
6  // ...
7
8  public function __construct(
```

```
 9 \Mlaphp\Request $request,
10 \Mlaphp\Response $response,
11 \Domain\Users\UserTransactions $user_transactions,
12 \Validator\NewUserValidator $validator
13 ) {
14 $this->request = $request;
15 $this->response = $response;
16 $this->user_transactions = $user_transactions;
17 $this->validator = $validator;
18 }
19
20 public function __invoke()
21 {
22 // ...
23 $user = $this->request->post['user'];
24
25 $this->validator->__invoke($user, $user_messages, $user_is_valid);
26
27 if ($user_is_valid) {
28 $this->user_transactions->addNewUser($user);
29 $this->response->setVars('success' => true);
30 } else {
31 $this->response->setVars(array(
32 'success' => false,
33 'user_messages' => $user_messages
34 ));
35 }
36
37 return $this->response;
38 }
39 }
40 ?>
```

Now we need to search the codebase and replace every instantiation of the modified class to pass the new dependency object. We run our tests as we go to make sure everything continues to operate properly.

Commit, Push, Notify QA

At this point we have either replaced a single `include` call, or multiple `include` calls to the same file. Because we have been testing along the way, we can now commit our new code and tests, push it all to common repository, and notify QA that we have new work for them to review.

Do ... While

We begin again by searching for the next `include` call in a class file. When all `include` calls have been replaced by class method invocations, we are done.

Common Questions

Can one class receive logic from many include files?

In the examples, we show the `include` code being extracted to a class by itself. If we have many related `include` files, it may be reasonable to collect them into the same class, each with their own method name. For example, the *NewUserValidator* logic might be only one of many user-related validators. We can reasonably imagine the class renamed as *UserValidator* with such methods as `validateNewUser()`, `validateExistingUser()`, and so on.

What about include calls originating in non-class files?

In our search for `include` calls, we look only in the `classes/` directory for the originating calls. It is likely that there are `include` calls that originate from other locations as well, such as the `views/`.

For the purposes of our refactoring, we don't particularly care about `include` calls that originate outside our classes. If an `include` is called only from non-class files, we can safely leave that `include` in its existing state.

Our main goal here is to remove `include` calls from class files, not necessarily from the entire legacy application. At this point, it is likely that most or all `include` calls outside our classes are part of the presentation logic anyway.

Review and next steps

After we have extracted all the include calls from our classes, we will have finally removed one of the last major artifacts of our legacy architecture. We can load a class without any side effects, and logic is executed only as a result of invoking a method. This is a big step forward for us.

We can now begin paying attention to overarching end-to-end architecture of our legacy application.

As things stand now, the entire legacy application is still located in the web server document root. Users browse to each page script directly. This means that the URLs are coupled to the file system. In addition, each page script has quite a bit of repeated logic: load a setup script, instantiate a controller using dependency injection, invoke the controller, and send the response.

Our next major goal, then, is to begin using a Front Controller in our legacy application. The front controller will be composed of some bootstrapping logic, a router, and a dispatcher. This will decouple our application from the file system and allow us to start removing our page scripts entirely.

But before we do so, we need to separate the public resources in our application from the non-public resources.

13
Separate Public and Non-Public Resources

At this point we have made major strides in reorganizing the core of our legacy application. However, the surrounding architecture still leaves much to be desired.

Among other things, our entire application is still embedded in the document root. This means that we need special protections on resources we intend to keep private, or that we need to rely on obscurity to make sure that clients do not browse to resources not intended to be public. Errors in web server configuration—or failure to attend to specific security measures—may reveal parts of our application to the public.

As such, our next step is to extract all public resources to a new document root. This will keep the non-public resources from being delivered by accident and will set up a structure for further refactoring.

Intermingled resources

Currently, our web server acts as a combined front controller, router, and dispatcher for our legacy application. The routes to the page scripts are mapped directly onto the file system, using the web server document root as a base. The web server document root, in turn, is mapped directly to the root of the legacy application.

For example, if the web server document root is `/var/www/htdocs`, it currently doubles as the application root. Thus, the URL path `/foo/bar.php` maps directly to `/var/www/htdocs/foo/bar.php`.

This may be fine for public resources, but there are large parts of our application that we do not want to be directly accessible by outsiders. For example, directories related to configuration and setup should not be exposed to possible outside examination. An error in the web server configuration may reveal the code itself, making our passwords and other information available to malicious users.

The separation process

Although the process itself is straightforward, the change we are making is a foundational one. It affects the server configuration as well as the legacy application structure. To fully effect this change, we will need to coordinate closely with any operations personnel who are in charge of server deployments.

In general, the process is as follows:

1. Coordinate with operations to communicate our intentions.
2. Create a new document root directory in our legacy application, along with a temporary index file.
3. Reconfigure the server to point to the new document root directory, and spot check the new configuration to see if our temporary index file appears.
4. Remove the temporary index file, then move all public resources to the new document root, and spot check along the way.
5. Commit, push, and coordinate with operations for QA testing.

Coordinate with operations personnel

This is the single most important step in the process. We should never make changes that affect server configurations without discussing our intentions with the people in charge of the servers (our operations personnel).

The feedback from operations will inform us as to the path we need to follow for making sure our change will be effective. They will advise or instruct us as to what the new document root directory name should be, along with what the new server configuration directives should be. They are the ones in charge of deploying the application, so we want to do our best to make their job as easy as possible. If operations is unhappy, then everyone will be unhappy.

Alternatively, if we have no operations personnel and are in charge of our own deployments, our job is both easier and harder. It is easier because we have no coordination and communication costs. It is harder because we need specific, detailed knowledge about server configurations. Proceed carefully in this case.

Create a document root directory

After coordinating with our operations personnel, we create a document root directory in the legacy application structure. Our operations contacts will have advised us on a proper directory name; in this case, let us assume that name is `docroot/`.

For example, if we currently have a legacy application structure that looks like this:

var/www/htdocs/

```
classes/
  ...
css/
  ...
foo/
    bar/
        baz.php
images/
  ...
includes/
  ...
index.php
js/
tests/
  ...
views/
  ...
```

... we add a new `docroot/` directory at the top level of the application. In the new document root directory, we add a temporary `index.html` file. This will let us know, later, if our server reconfiguration works properly. It can contain any text we like, such as `Rejoice! The new configuration works!`.

When we are done, the new directory structure will look something more like this:

/var/www/htdocs/

```
classes/
  ...
css/
  ...
docroot/
    index.html
foo/
    bar/
        baz.php
```

```
images/
  ...
includes/
  ...
index.php
    js/
  ...
tests/
  ...
views/
  ...
```

Reconfigure the server

We now reconfigure our local development web server to point to the new `docroot/` directory. Our operations personnel should have given us some instructions on how to do this.

In Apache, we might edit the configuration file for our local development environment to change the `DocumentRoot` directive in a related `.conf` file from the main application directory:

```
DocumentRoot "/var/www/htdocs"
```

... to our newly created subdirectory within the application:

```
DocumentRoot "/var/www/htdocs/docroot"
```

We then save the file, and reload or restart the server to apply our changes.

> The applicable `DocumentRoot` directive may be in one of many locations. It could be in the main `httpd.conf` file, or perhaps inside a separate configuration file as part of a `VirtualHost` directive. If we are using something other than Apache, the configuration is probably in an entirely different file. Unfortunately, it is beyond the scope of this book to give full instructions on web server administration. Please review the documentation for your particular server for more information.

Once we have applied our configuration changes, we browse to our legacy application to see if the new document root is being honored. We should see the contents of our temporary `index.html` file. If not, we have done something wrong and need to revisit our changes until they work as expected.

Move public resources

Now that we have configured the web server to point to our new `docroot/` directory, we can safely remove our temporary `index.html` file.

After doing so, our next step is to move all of our public resources from their current locations into the new `docroot/` directory. This includes all of our page scripts, style sheets, JavaScript files, images, and so on. It does *not* include anything that users should not be able to browse to: classes, includes, setup, configuration, command-line scripts, tests, view files, and so forth.

We want to maintain the same relative location in `docroot/` as they had when in the base of the application, so we should not change file names or directory names when moving.

As we move our public resources to their new location, we should occasionally spot check our modified structure by browsing through the application. This will help us discover any problems with our changes earlier rather than later.

> Some of our moved PHP files may still depend on `include` files in specific locations. In these cases, we may need to modify them to point to paths relative to our new `docroot/` directory. Alternatively, we may need to modify our include-path values so that they can find the necessary files.

When we are done, we will have a directory structure that looks a little more like this:

/var/www/htdocs/

```
classes/
  ...
docroot/
   css/
       ...
   foo/
      bar/
         baz.php

   index.php
   js/
     ...
   images/
     ...
includes/
```

```
      . . .
   tests/
      . . .
   views/
      . . .
```

Commit, push, coordinate

When we have moved all of our public resources to the new `docroot/` directory and the legacy application works properly in this new structure, we commit all of our changes and push them to the common repository.

At this point, we would normally notify QA of our changes for them to test. However, because we have made a foundational change to the server configuration, we need to coordinate the QA testing with our operations personnel. Operations will probably need to deploy the new configuration to the QA servers. Only then will QA be able to effectively check our work.

Common Questions

Is This Really Necessary?

Most of the time it seems harmless to leave the various non-public resources in the document root. But for our next step, it is going to be very important that we have a separation between our public resources and our non-public ones.

Review and next steps

We have now begun to refactor the overarching architecture of our legacy application. By creating a document root that separates our public resources from non-public ones, we can start to put together a front-controller system to control access to our application.

14
Decouple URL Paths from File Paths

Even though we have a document root that separates our public and non-public resources, the users of our legacy application still browse directly to our page scripts. This means that our URLs are coupled directly to file system paths on the web server.

Our next step is to decouple the paths so that we can route URLs independently to any target we want. This means putting in place a Front Controller to handle all incoming requests for our legacy application.

Coupled Paths

As we noted in the previous chapter, our web server acts as a combined front controller, router, and dispatcher for our legacy application. The routes to the page scripts are still mapped directly onto the file system, using our `docroot/` directory as the base for all URL paths.

This presents us with some structural problems. For example, if we want to expose a new or different URL, we have to modify the location of the related page script in the file system. Similarly, we cannot change what page script responds to a particular URL. There is no way intercept the incoming request before it is routed.

These and other problems, including the ability to complete future refactorings, mean that we must create a single entry point for all incoming requests. This entry point is called a front controller.

In our first implementation of a front controller for our legacy application, we will add a Router to convert the incoming URL path to a page script path. That will allow us to remove our page scripts from the document root, thereby decoupling the URLs from the file system.

The Decoupling Process

As with separating our public resources from our non-public ones, we will have to make a change to our web server configuration. Specifically, we will enable URL rewriting so we can point all incoming requests to a front controller. We need to coordinate this refactoring with our operations personnel so they can deploy the changes as easily as possible.

The process, in general, is as follows:

1. Coordinate with operations to communicate our intentions.
2. Create a front controller script in the document root.
3. Create a `pages/` directory for our page scripts, along with a `page not found` page script and controller.
4. Reconfigure the web server to enable URL rewriting.
5. Spot check the reconfigured web server to make sure the front controller and URL rewriting work properly.
6. Move all page scripts from `docroot/` to `pages/`, spot checking along the way.
7. Commit, push, and coordinate with operations for QA testing.

Coordinate with Operations

This is the single most important step in the process. We should never make changes that affect server configurations without discussing our intentions with the people in charge of the servers (i.e., our operations personnel).

In this case, we need to tell our operations personnel that we have to enable URL rewriting. They will advise or instruct us on how to do this for our particular web server.

Alternatively, if we have no operations personnel and are in charge of our own servers, we will need to determine on our own how to enable URL rewriting. Proceed carefully in this case.

Add a Front Controller

Once we have coordinated with our operations personnel, we will add a front controller script. We will also add a `page not found` script, controller, and view.

First, we create the front controller script in our document root. It uses a `Router` class to map the incoming URL to a page script. We call it front.php, or some other name that indicates it is a front controller:

```
docroot/front.php
1 <?php
2 // the router class file
3 require dirname(__DIR__) . '/classes/Mlaphp/Router.php';
4
5 // set up the router
6 $pages_dir = dirname(__DIR__) . '/pages';
7 $router = new \Mlaphp\Router($pages_dir);
8
9 // match against the url path
10 $path = parse_url($_SERVER['REQUEST_URI'], PHP_URL_PATH);
11 $route = $router->match($path);
12
13 // require the page script
14 require $route;
15 ?>
```

> We require the `Router` class file because the autoloader has not been registered yet. That will happen only when we execute the page script, which does not occur until the end of the front controller logic. We will remedy this situation in the next chapter.

Create a pages/ Directory

The front controller references a `$pages_dir`. The idea is that we will move all our page scripts out of the document root and into this new directory.

First, we make a `pages/` directory at the top level of our legacy application, next to the `classes/`, `docroot/`, `views/`, etc. directories.

We then create a `pages/not-found.php` script, along with a corresponding controller and view file. The front controller will call the `not-found.php` script when the `Router` is unable to match a URL path. The `not-found.php` script should set itself up like any other page script in our legacy application, then invoke its corresponding view file for the response:

```
pages/not-found.php
1 <?php
2 require '../includes/setup.php';
3
```

```
 4 $request = new \Mlaphp\Request($GLOBALS);
 5 $response = new \Mlaphp\Response('/path/to/app/views');
 6 $controller = new \Controller\NotFound($request, $response);
 7
 8 $response = $controller->__invoke();
 9
10 $response->send();
11 ?>
```

classes/Controller/NotFound.php

```
 1 <?php
 2 namespace Controller;
 3
 4 use Mlaphp\Request;
 5 use Mlaphp\Response;
 6
 7 class NotFound
 8 {
 9 protected $request;
10
11 protected $response;
12
13 public function __construct(Request $request, Response $response)
14 {
15 $this->request = $request;
16 $this->response = $response;
17 }
18
19 public function __invoke()
20 {
21 $url_path = parse_url(
22 $this->request->server['REQUEST_URI'],
23 PHP_URL_PATH
24 );
25
26 $this->response->setView('not-found.html.php');
27 $this->response->setVars(array(
28 'url_path' => $url_path,
29 ));
30
31 return $this->response;
32 }
33 }
34 ?>
```

views/not-found.html.php
```
1 <?php $this->header('HTTP/1.1 404 Not Found'); ?>
2 <html>
3 <head>
4 <title>Not Found</title>
5 </head>
6 <body>
7 <h1>Not Found</h1>
8 <p><?php echo $this->esc($url_path); ?></p>
9 </body>
10 </html>
```

Reconfigure the Server

Now that we have our front controller in place and a target location for our page scripts, we reconfigure our local development web server to enable URL rewriting. Our operations personnel should have given us some instructions on how to do this.

> Unfortunately, it is beyond the scope of this book to give full instructions on web server administation. Please review the documentation for your particular server for more information.

In Apache, we would first enable the mod_rewrite module. In some Linux distributions, this is as easy as issuing sudo a2enmod rewrite. In others, we need to edit the httpd.conf file to enable it.

Once URL rewriting is enabled, we need to instruct the web server to point all incoming requests to our front controller. In Apache, we might add a docroot/.htaccess file to our legacy application. Alternatively, we may modify one of the Apache configuration files for our local development server. The rewriting logic would look like the following:

docroot/.htaccess
```
1 # enable rewriting
2 RewriteEngine On
3
4 # turn empty requests into requests for the "front.php"
5 # bootstrap script, keeping the query string intact
6 RewriteRule ^$ front.php [QSA]
7
8 # for all files and dirs not in the document root,
9 # reroute to the "front.php" bootstrap script,
10 # keeping the query string intact, and making this
11 # the last rewrite rule
```

```
12 RewriteCond %{REQUEST_FILENAME} !-f
13 RewriteCond %{REQUEST_FILENAME} !-d
14 RewriteRule ^(.*)$ front.php [QSA,L]
```

> For example, if the incoming request is for /foo/bar/baz.php,
> the web server will invoke the front.php script instead. This will
> be the case for every request. The various superglobals values will
> remain unchanged, so $_SERVER['REQUEST_URI'] will still
> indicate /foo/bar/baz.php.
>
> Finally, after we have enabled URL rewriting, we restart or reload
> the web server to make our changes take effect.

Spot check

Now that we have enabled URL rewriting to point all requests to our new front
controller, we should browse to our legacy application, using a URL path that
we know does not exist. The front controller should show us the output from our
not-found.php page script. This indicates that our changes are working properly.
If not, we need to review and revise our changes up to this point and try to fix
whatever went wrong.

Move Page scripts

Once we are sure that the URL rewriting and front controller are operating properly,
we can begin to move all of our pages scripts out of docroot/ and into our new
pages/ directory. Note that we are moving only page scripts. We should leave all the
other resources in docroot/, including the front.php front controller.

For example, if we start out with this structure:

```
/path/to/app/
docroot/
css/
foo/
bar/
baz.php
front.php
images/
index.php
js/
pages/
not-found.php
```

We should end up with this structure instead:

```
/path/to/app/
docroot/
css/
front.php
images/
js/
pages/
foo/
bar/
baz.php
index.php
not-found.php
```

We have moved only the page scripts. Images, CSS files, Javascript files, and the front controller all remain in `docroot/`.

Because we are moving files around, we may need to change our include-path values to point to the new relative directory locations.

As we move each file or directory from `docroot/` to `pages/`, we should spot check our changes to make sure the legacy application continues to work correctly.

Due to the rewriting rules described earlier, our page scripts should continue to work whether they are in `docroot/` or `pages/`. We want to make sure to move all page scripts to `pages/` before we continue.

Commit, Push, Coordinate

When we have moved all of our page scripts to the new `pages/` directory, and our legacy application works properly in this new structure, we commit all of our changes and push them to the common repository.

At this point, we would normally notify QA of our changes for them to test. However, because we have made a change to the server configuration, we need to coordinate the QA testing with our operations personnel. Operations will probably need to deploy the new configuration to the QA servers. Only then will QA be able to effectively check our work.

Common Questions

Did we really Decouple the Paths?

Astute observers will note that our *Router* still uses the incoming URL path to find the page scripts. The only difference between this and the original setup is that the path is mapped onto the pages/ directory instead of the docroot/ directory. Have we actually decoupled the URLs from the file system after all?

Yes, we have achieved our decoupling goal. This is because we now have an interception point between the URL path and the page script that gets executed. Using the *Router*, we could create an array of routes where URL paths are the keys and file paths are values. That mapping array would allow us to route the incoming URL path to any page script we like.

For example, if we want to map a URL path like /foo/bar.php to a page script like /baz/dib.php, we could do so via the setRoutes() method on the *Router*:

```
1 $router->setRoutes(array(
2 '/foo/bar.php' => '/baz/dib.php',
3 ));
```

Then when we match() the incoming URL path of /foo/bar.php against the *Router*, our returned route will be /baz/dib.php. We can then execute that route as the page script for the incoming URL. We will use a variation on this technique in the next chapter.

Review and next steps

With the decoupling of our URLs from our page scripts, we are nearly finished with our modernization work. Only two refactorings remain. First, we will move repeated logic in our page scripts up to the front controller. Then we will remove the page scripts entirely and replace them with a dependency injection container.

15
Remove Repeated Logic in Page Scripts

As things are now, the logic in our page scripts is highly repetitive. They all look very similar. Each one loads a setup script, instantiates a series of dependencies for a page controller, invokes that controller, and sends the response.

Our front controller gives us a place where we can execute the common elements of each page script and remove that repetition. Once the repetition has been removed, we can begin to eliminate the page scripts themselves.

Repeated logic

In essence, each of our page scripts follows this organizational flow:

```
Generic Page Script
1 <?php
2 // one or more identical setup scripts
3 require 'setup.php';
4
5 // a series of dependencies to build a controller
6 $request = new \Mlaphp\Request($GLOBALS);
7 $response = new \Mlaphp\Response('/path/to/app/views');
8 $controller = new \Controller\PageName($request, $response);
9
10 // invoke the controller and send the response
11 $response = $controller->__invoke();
12 $response->send();
13 ?>
```

Because we have been diligent about always using the same variable name for our controller object ($controller), always using the same method name for invoking it (__invoke()), and always using the same variable name for the response ($response), we can see that the only part of each page script that is different is the central section. That central block builds the controller object. Everything before and after is identical.

Further, because we have a front controller to handle all incoming requests, we now have a place to put the common before and after logic of every page script. That is what we will do here.

The Removal Process

In general, the removal process is as follows:

1. Modify the front controller to add setup, controller invocation, and response sending.

2. Modify each page script to remove the setup, controller invocation, and response sending.

3. Spot check, commit, push, and notify QA.

Modify the Front controller

First, we modify the front controller logic to perform the logic common to every page script. We change it from the code listed in the previous chapter to something more like this:

docroot/front.php
```
1 <?php
2 // page script setup
3 require dirname(__DIR__) . '/includes/setup.php';
4
5 // set up the router
6 $pages_dir = dirname(__DIR__) . '/pages';
7 $router = new \Mlaphp\Router($pages_dir);
8
9 // match against the url path
10 $path = parse_url($_SERVER['REQUEST_URI'], PHP_URL_PATH);
11 $route = $router->match($path);
12
13 // require the page script
14 require $route;
15
```

```
16 // invoke the controller and send the response
17 $response = $controller->__invoke();
18 $response->send();
19 ?>
```

We have replaced the line that requires the `Router` class file with a line that requires the setup script. (Way back in the chapter on autoloading, we put the autoloader into our setup script, so it should be autoloading the `Router` class for us now.)

We have also added two lines after requiring the file `$route` to the page script. These invoke the controller and set the response. We use the common variable names for the controller and response objects in this shared logic. (If you chose something other than `$controller` and `$response` in the page scripts, replace those in the above script. Similarly, if you used a common controller method other than `__invoke()`, replace that as well.)

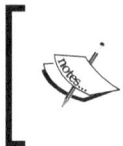

> Note that the setup work is going to be specific to our legacy application. As long as the setup work is the same for every page script (which it should be at this point) placing the common setup work here will be just fine.

Remove Logic from Page Scripts

Now that we have added setup, controller invocation, and response-sending work to the front controller, we can remove that same work from each page script. Doing so should be as easy as doing a project-wide search in the `pages/` directory and deleting the found lines.

Finding the setup lines probably requires a regular expression, since the relative location of the setup scripts may result in lines that use relative directory traversals. The following regular expression will find `includes/setup.php`, `../includes/setup.php`, `dirname(__DIR__) . /includes/setup.php`, and so on:

Search for setup:

```
1 ^\s*(require|require_once|include|include_once) .*includes/setup\.
php.*$
```

However, finding the controller invocation and response-sending lines should not require a regular expression, since they should be identical in every page script.

Search for controller invocation ...

```
1 $response = $controller->__invoke();
```

Search for response sending …

```
1 $response->send();
```

In each case, delete the found line. It is no longer needed now that the logic has been moved to the front controller.

Spot Check, Commit, Push, Notify QA

Once the repeated page script logic has been removed in favor of the same logic placed in the front controller, we can spot check the application. We do so by running our characterization tests if they exist, or by browsing to or otherwise invoking each page in the application if they do not.

After we are sure that the application still works properly, we commit our new code and push it to the common repository. Then we notify QA that we have new work for them to review.

Common Questions

What if the Setup Work Is Inconsistent?

In the examples throughout this book, we have shown only a single script doing the setup work for each page script. Some legacy applications may use more than one setup script. As long as the setup work is identical across each page script, even if it is composed of more than one script, then we can move all the setup work to the front controller.

However, if the setup work is not identical across each page script, we have a problem to deal with. If the page scripts do not enjoy an indentical setup process at this point, we should do what we can to address that before continuing.

It is imperative that we make the setup work identical in all page scripts. This may mean including all the different setup work from all page scripts in the front controller, even if some scripts don't need all that setup work. We can remedy this overlap the next chapter if necessary.

If we cannot enforce an identical single-stage setup process, we may have to pursue a dual or two-stage setup process. First, we consolidate common setup work into the front controller and remove it from the page scripts. Extraneous, special-case, or page-specific setup work can remain with the page script as a degenerate but necessary part of the dependency creation work.

What if we used inconsistent naming?

In previous chapters, this book emphasizes the importance of consistent naming. This chapter is the point at which that consistency pays off.

If we discover we have been inconsistent in our naming of the controller object variable and/or the controller method name, all is not lost. We will not be able to do a one-pass search-and-replace, but we can still work through each page script manually and change the names to be consistent. Then the newly consistent names can be used by the front controller.

Review and next steps

With this step, we have reduced our page scripts to a bare core of logic. All they do now is set up dependencies for, and then create, a controller object. The front controller does everything before that, and everything after.

As it happens, even this logic can be extracted from the page scripts. An object called a dependency injection container can receive the object creation logic as series of closures, one closure per page script. The container can handle the object creation for us and we can remove the page scripts entirely.

Thus, our final refactoring will extract all object creation logic to a dependency injection container. We will also modify our front controller to instantiate controller objects instead of requiring page scripts. In doing so, we will have removed all of our page scripts and our application will have a fully modernized architecture.

16
Add a Dependency Injection Container

We have reached the final step in our modernization process. We will remove the last vestiges of our page scripts by moving their remaining logic into a dependency injection container. The container will be responsible for coordinating all the object creation activity in our application. In doing so, we will modify our front controller again, and begin adding routes that point to controller classes instead of file paths.

> For this final step in the modernization process, it is best if we have PHP 5.3 or later installed. This is because we need closures for critical parts of the application logic. If we do not have access to PHP 5.3, there is a less viable but still workable option for implementing a dependency injection container. We address that situation as the last of the "Common Questions" in this chapter.

What is a Dependency Injection Container?

Dependency injection as a technique is something we have been practicing since early in this book. To reiterate, the idea behind dependency injection is that we push depependencies into an object from the outside. This is as opposed to creating dependency objects while inside a class via the new keyword, or reaching out of the current scope to bring in dependencies via the `globals` keyword.

> For an overview of inversion of control in general and dependency injection in specific, read Fowler's article on containers at `http://martinfowler.com/articles/injection.html`.

To accomplish our dependency injection activities, we have been manually creating the necessary objects in a page script. For any object that needed a dependency, we created that dependency first, then we created the object that depended on it and passed in the dependency. This creation process has sometimes been deeply layered, as when the dependencies have dependencies. Regardless of the complexity and depth, the logic for doing so is currently embedded in page scripts.

The idea behind a dependency injection *container* is to keep all that object creation logic in a single place, so that we are no longer required to use a page script to set up our objects. We can place each piece of object creation logic in the container under a unique name, called a service.

We can then tell the container to return a new instance of any defined service object. Alternatively, we can tell the container to create and return a shared instance of that service object, so that each time we get it, it is always the same instance. Careful combinations of new instances and shared instances of container services will allow us to pare down our dependency creation logic.

> At no point will we be passing the container into any of the objects that need dependencies. To do so would be using a pattern called Service Locator. We avoid Service Locator activity because doing so is a violation of scope. When the container is inside an object, and that object uses it to retrieve dependencies, we are only one step removed from where we started; that is, with the `global` keyword. As such, we do not pass the container around -- it stays entirely outside the scope of the objects it creates.

There are many different container implementations in PHP land, each with its own strengths and weaknesses. To keep things tailored to our modernization process, we will use the *Mlaphp\Di*. This is a stripped down container implementation that is well-suited to our transitional needs.

Adding a DI Container

The process for adding a DI container, in general, is as follows:

1. Add a new `services.php` include file to create the container and manage its services.

2. Define a `router` service in the container.

3. Modify the front controller to include the `services.php` file and use the `router` service, then spot check the application.

4. Extract creation logic from each page script to the container:

   1. Create a service in the container named for the page script controller class.

   2. Copy the logic from the page script into the container service. Rename variables as needed to use DI container properties.

   3. Route the page URL path to the container service name (i.e., the controller name).

   4. Spot check and commit the change.

   5. Continue until all page scripts have been extracted to the container.

5. Remove the empty `pages/` directory, commit, push, and notify QA.

Add a DI Container Include File

To keep our existing setup files from growing even larger, we will introduce a new `services.php` setup file. Yes, this means adding another `include` to the front controller, but if we have been diligent, there are few if any includes remaining in our application. This one will be of little import.

First, we need to pick an appropriate location for the file. It is probably best if it goes along with any other setup files we already have, perhaps in an existing `includes/` directory.

Then we create the file with the following line. (We will add much more to this file as we continue.) Because the file will be loaded as the last of our setup files, we can presume that autoloading will be active, so there is no need to load the `Di` class file:

includes/services.php

```
1 <?php
2 $di = new \Mlaphp\Di($GLOBALS);
3 ?>
```

What happens as a result is that the new `$di` instance is loaded with all the existing global variable values. These values are retained as properties on the container. For example, if our setup files create a `$db_user` variable, we can now additionally access that value as `$di->db_user`. These are copies, not references, so changes to one will not affect the other.

> **Why do we retain the existing variables as properties?**
>
> Currently, our page scripts access the global variables directly for their creation work. However, in a later step, the creation logic will no longer be in the global scope. It will be "inside" the DI container. Thus, we populate the DI container with a copy of the variables that would have been available otherwise.

Add a Router Service

Now that we have a DI container in place, let's add our first service.

Recall that the purpose of a DI container is to create objects for us. Currently, the front controller creates a *Router* object, so we will add a router service to the container. (In the next step, we will have the front controller use this service instead of creating a *Router* on its own.)

In the services.php file, add the following lines:

includes/services.php

```php
1 <?php
2 // set a container service for the router
3 $di->set('router', function () use ($di) {
4 $router = new \Mlaphp\Router('/path/to/app/pages');
5 $router->setRoutes(array());
6 return $router;
7 });
8 ?>
```

Let's examine the service defintion a little bit.

- The service name is router. We will use all-lowercase names for service objects intended to be created once as shared instances, and fully-qualified class names for service objects intended to be created as new instances each time. Thus, in this case, our intent is that only a single shared router will be available via the container. (This is a convention, not a rule that is enforced by the container.)

- The service definition is a callable. In this case, it is a closure. The closure receives no parameters, but it does use the $di object from the current scope. This makes it possible for the definition code to access container properties and other container services while building the service object.

- We create and then return the object represented by the service name. We do not need to check if the object already exists in the container; the container internals will do that for us if we ask for a shared instance.

With this bit of code, the container now knows how to create a `router` service. It is lazy-loaded code that will only be executed when we call `$di->newInstance()` (to get a new instance of the service object) or `$di->get()` (to get a shared instance of the service object).

Modify the Front Controller

Now that we have a DI container and a `router` service definition, we modify the front controller to load the container and use the `router` service.

```
docroot/front.php
1 <?php
2 require dirname(__DIR__) . '/includes/setup.php';
3 require dirname(__DIR__) . '/includes/services.php';
4
5 // get the shared router service
6 $router = $di->get('router');
7
8 // match against the url path
9 $path = parse_url($_SERVER['REQUEST_URI'], PHP_URL_PATH);
10 $route = $router->match($path);
11
12 // container service, or page script?
13 if ($di->has($route)) {
14 // create a new $controller instance
15 $controller = $di->newInstance($route);
16 } else {
17 // require the page script
18 require $route;
19 }
20
21 // invoke the controller and send the response
22 $response = $controller->__invoke();
23 $response->send();
24 ?>
```

We have made the following changes from the previous implementation:

* We added a `require` for the `services.php` container file as the very last of our setup includes.

* Instead of creating a *Router* object directly, we `get()` a shared instance of the `router` service object from the `$di` container.

- We have changed our dispatching logic somewhat. After we get a $route from the $router, we check to see if the $di container has() a matching service. If so, it treats the $route as a service name for a new $controller instance; otherwise, it treats the $route as a file in pages/ that creates a $controller. Either way, the code then invokes the controller and sends the response.

After these changes, we spot check the application to make sure the new router service works properly. If it does not, we undo and redo our changes up to this point until the application works as it did before.

We may wish to commit our changes once the application works. This is so that if future changes go bad, we have a known-working state to which we can revert.

Extract Page Scripts to Services

Now comes the final push in modernizing our legacy application. We are going to remove our page scripts one-by-one and put their logic into the container.

Create a Container Service

Pick any page script and determine what class it uses to create its $controller instance. Then, in the DI container, create an empty service definition for that class name.

For example, if we have this page script:

pages/articles.php

```
1  <?php
2  $db = new Database($db_host, $db_user, $db_pass);
3  $articles_gateway = new ArticlesGateway($db);
4  $users_gateway = new UsersGateway($db);
5  $article_transactions = new ArticleTransactions(
6  $articles_gateway,
7  $users_gateway
8  );
9  $response = new \Mlaphp\Response('/path/to/app/views');
10 $controller = new \Controller\ArticlesPage(
11 $request,
12 $response,
13 $user,
14 $article_transactions
15 );
16 ?>
```

We the controller class being instantiated is `Controller\ArticlesPage`. In our `services.php` file, we create an empty service definition with that name:

includes/services.php
```php
1  <?php
2  $di->set('Controller\ArticlesPage', function () use ($di) {
3  });
4  ?>
```

Next, we move the page script setup logic into the service definition. When we do so, we should note any variables that we expected from the global scope, and prefix them with `$di->` to reference the appropriate container properties. (Recall that these were loaded from `$GLOBALS` early in the `services.php` file.) We also return the controller instance at the end of the definition.

When we are done, the service definition will look something like this:

includes/services.php
```php
1  <?php
2  $di->set('Controller\ArticlesPage', function () use ($di) {
3  // replace `$variables` with `$di->` properties
4  $db = new Database($di->db_host, $di->db_user, $di->db_pass);
5  // create dependencies
6  $articles_gateway = new ArticlesGateway($db);
7  $users_gateway = new UsersGateway($db);
8  $article_transactions = new ArticleTransactions(
9  $articles_gateway,
10 $users_gateway
11 );
12 $response = new \Mlaphp\Response('/path/to/app/views');
13 // return the new instance
14 return new \Controller\ArticlesPage(
15 $request,
16 $response,
17 $user,
18 $article_transactions
19 );
20 });
21 ?>
```

Once we have copied the logic over to the container, we delete the orginal page script file from `pages/`.

Route the URL Path to the Container Service

Now that we have removed the page script in favor of the container service, we need to make sure the *Router* points to the container service instead of the now-missing page script. We do this by adding an array element to the setRoutes() method parameter where the key is the URL path and the value is the service name.

For example, if the URL path is /articles.php and our new container service is named Controller\ArticlesPage, we would modify our router service like so:

```
includes/services.php
1  <?php
2  // ...
3  $di->set('router', function () use ($di) {
4  $router = new \Mlaphp\Router($di->pages_dir);
5  $router->setRoutes(array(
6  // add a route that points to a container service name
7  '/articles.php' => 'Controller\ArticlesPage',
8  ));
9  return $router;
10 });
11 ?>
```

Spot Check and Commit

Finally, we check to see if the conversion from page script to container service works as we expect. We spot check the URL path to the old page script by browsing to or otherwise invoking that URL. If it works, then we know the container service has successfully taken the place of the now-deleted page script.

If not, we need to undo and redo our changes to see where things went wrong. The most common errors I see here are:

- Failure to replace $var variables in the page script with $di->var properties in the service definition
- Failure to return the object from the service definition
- Mismatches between the controller service name and the mapped route value

Once we are sure the application routes the URL to the new container service, and that the service works properly, we commit our changes.

Do ... While

We proceed to the next page script and begin the process over again. When all page scripts have been converted to container services and then deleted, we are done.

Remove pages/, Commit, Push, Notify QA

After we have extracted all of our page scripts to the DI container, the `pages/` directory should be empty. We can now safely remove it.

With that, we commit our work, push to the common repository, and notify QA that we have new changes for them to review.

Common Questions

How can we refine our service definitions?

When we are done extracting our object creation logic to the container, each service definition is likely to be rather long, and probably repetitive. It would be nice to reduce the repetition and refine the service definition so as to make them short and succinct. We can do so by further extracting each part of object creation logic to its own service.

For example, if we have several services that use a *Request* object, we can extract the object creation logic to its own service and then reference that service in other services. We can name it to show our intent that it be used as can be intended as a shared service (`request`) or as a new instance (`Mlaphp\Request`). Other services can then use `get()` or `newInstance()` instead of creating the request internally.

Given our earlier `Controller\ArticlesPage` service, we could split it up into several reusable services like so:

```
includes/services.php
1  <?php
2  // ...
3
4  $di->set('request', function () use ($di) {
5  return new \Mlaphp\Request($GLOBALS);
6  });
7
8  $di->set('response', function () use ($di) {
9  return new \Mlaphp\Response('/path/to/app/views');
10 });
11
```

```
12 $di->set('database', function () use ($di) {
13 return new \Database(
14 $di->db_host,
15 $di->db_user,
16 $di->db_pass
17 );
18 });
19
20 $di->set('Domain\Articles\ArticlesGateway', function () use ($di) {
21 return new \Domain\Articles\ArticlesGateway($di->get('database'));
22 });
23
24 $di->set('Domain\Users\UsersGateway', function () use ($di) {
25 return new \Domain\Users\UsersGateway($di->get('database'));
26 });
27
28 $di->set('Domain\Articles\ArticleTransactions', function () use
($di) {
29 return new \Domain\Articles\ArticleTransactions(
30 $di->newInstance('Domain\Articles\ArticlesGateway'),
31 $di->newInstance('Domain\Users\UsersGateway'),
32 );
33 });
34
35 $di->set('Controller\ArticlesPage', function () use ($di) {
36 return new \Controller\ArticlesPage(
37 $di->get('request'),
38 $di->get('response'),
39 $di->user,
40 $di->newInstance('Domain\Articles\ArticleTransactions')
41 );
42 });
43 ?>
```

Notice how the `Controller\ArticlesPage` service now references other services in the container to build its own object. When we get a new instance of the `Controller\ArticlesPage` service object, it addresses the `$di` container to obtain the shared request and response objects, the `$user` property, and a new instance of the *ArticleTransactions* service object. That, in turn, recursively addresses the `$di` container to obtain the dependencies for that service object, and so on.

What if there are includes In the Page Script?

Even though we have done our best to remove them, it is possible that we still have some include files in our page scripts. When we copy the page script logic to the container, we have little choice but to copy them as well. However, once all our page scripts have been converted to the container, we can look for commonalities and begin extracting the include logic either to a setup script or to separate classes (which themselves can become services if needed).

Can we reduce the size of the services.php file?

Depending on the number of page scripts in our application, our DI container may end up with tens or hundreds of service definitions. This can be a lot to manage or scan through in a single file.

If we like, it is perfectly reasonable to split the container into multiple files, and make the services.php a series of include calls to bring in the various definitions.

Can we reduce the size of the router service?

As a subset of the DI container file length, the router service in particluar is likely to become very long. This is because we map every URL in the application to a service; if there are hundreds of URLs, there will be hundreds of router lines.

As an alternative, we can create a separate routes.php file and have it return an array of routes. We can then include that file in the setRoutes() call:

includes/routes.php
```
1 <?php return array(
2 '/articles.php' => 'Controller\ArticlesPage',
3 ); ?>
```

includes/services.php
```
1 <?php
2 // ...
3 $di->set('router', function () use ($di) {
4 $router = new \Mlaphp\Router($di->pages_dir);
5 $router->setRoutes(include '/path/to/includes/routes.php');
6 return $router;
7 });
8 ?>
```

That at least will reduce the size of the services.php file, even though it does not reduce the size of the routes array.

What if we cannot update to PHP 5.3?

The examples in this chapter show a DI container that uses closures to encapsulate object creation logic. Closures only became available in PHP 5.3, so if we are stuck on an earlier version of PHP, it looks like using a DI container is simply not an option.

This turns out not to be true. With some extra effort and a greater toleration for inelegance, we can still build a DI container for PHP 5.2 and earlier.

First, we need to extend the DI container so that we can add methods to it. Then, instead of creating service definitions as closures, we create them as methods on our extended container:

classes/Di.php
```
1  <?php
2  class Di extends \Mlaphp\Di
3  {
4  public function database()
5  {
6  return new \Database(
7  $this->db_host,
8  $this->db_user,
9  $this->db_pass
10  );
11  }
12  }
13  ?>
```

(Notice how we use `$this` instead of `$di` in the method.)

Then in our `services.php` file, the callable becomes a reference to this method, instead of an inline closure:

includes/services.php
```
1  <?php
2  $di->set('database', array($di, 'database'));
3  ?>
```

This is messy but workable. It can also get pretty verbose. Our earlier example of splitting up the `Controller\ArticlesPage` ends up looking more like this:

includes/services.php
```
1  <?php
2  // ...
3  $di->set('request', array($di, 'request'));
4  $di->set('response', array($di, 'response'));
5  $di->set('database', array($di, 'database'));
```

```
6 $di->set('Domain\Articles\ArticlesGateway', array($di,
'ArticlesGateway'));
7 $di->set('Domain\Users\UsersGateway', array($di, 'UsersGateway'));
8 $di->set(
9 'Domain\Articles\ArticleTransactions',
10 array($di, 'ArticleTransactions')
11 );
12 $di->set('Controller\ArticlesPage', array($di, 'ArticlesPage'));
13 ?>
```

classes/Di.php

```
1 <?php
2 class Di extends \Mlaphp\Di
3 {
4 public function request()
5 {
6 return new \Mlaphp\Request($GLOBALS);
7 }
8
9 public function response()
10 {
11 return new \Mlaphp\Response('/path/to/app/views');
12 }
13
14 public function database()
15 {
16 return new \Database(
17 $this->db_host,
18 $this->db_user,
19 $this->db_pass
20 );
21 }
22
23 public function ArticlesGateway()
24 {
25 return new \Domain\Articles\ArticlesGateway($this-
>get('database'));
26 }
27
28 public function UsersGateway()
29 {
30 return new \Domain\Users\UsersGateway($this->get('database'));
31 }
32
33 public function ArticleTransactions()
```

```
34 {
35 return new \Domain\Articles\ArticleTransactions(
36 $this->newInstance('ArticlesGateway'),
37 $this->newInstance('UsersGateway'),
38 );
39 }
40
41 public function ArticlesPage()
42 {
43 return new \Controller\ArticlesPage(
44 $this->get('request'),
45 $this->get('response'),
46 $this->user,
47 $this->newInstance('ArticleTransactions')
48 );
49 }
50 }
51 ?>
```

Unfortunately, we may have to break with some of our style conventions to keep the service names looking like their related method names. We also have to shorten the service method names intended for new instances down to their ending class names, instead of their fully qualified names. Otherwise we find ourselves with overly long and confusing method names.

This can get confusing fast, but it does work. In all, it really is better if we can upgrade to PHP 5.3 or later.

Review and next steps

At last, we have completed our modernization process. We no longer have any page scripts. All of our application logic has been converted to classes, and the only remaining include files are part of the bootstrap and setup process. All of our object creation logic exists inside a container, where we can modify it directly without having to disturb the internals of our objects.

What could the next step possibly be after this? The answer is continuous improvement and it is going to last for the rest of your career.

17
Conclusion

Let us think back on our progress.

We started out with a spaghetti mess of a legacy application. The entire application was based in the document root, and users browsed directly to page scripts. It used an include-oriented architecture, where merely including a file caused logic to be executed. Global variables were scattered everywhere, which made debugging difficult to impossible. There were no tests of any sort, much less unit tests, so every change raised the possibility of breaking something else. There was no clear separation of model, view, and controller layers. SQL statements were embedded throughout our code, and domain logic was mixed in with presentation and action logic.

Now, after a great deal of effort, dedication, and commitment, we have modernized our legacy application. The document root consists only of public resources and a front controller. All the page scripts have been distilled into separate model, view, and controller layers. These layers are represented by a well-structured series of classes, each with its own set of unit tests. The application objects are built inside a dependency injection container, keeping their operation separate from their creation.

What could possibly be left to do?

Opportunities for improvement

Even though we have modernized our application, it is still not perfect. Frankly, it will *never* be perfect (whatever that may happen to mean). There will always be some opportunity to improve it. Indeed, the modernization process itself has revealed many opportunities for us.

- The data source layer is composed of a series of Gateways. While they serve our purpose nicely for now, it may be better to restructure these as Data Mappers that interact more cleanly with our domain objects.

- The domain layer is built on top of Transaction Scripts. These, too, are fine in their own way, but as we work with them, we may realize that they are insufficient for our needs. They combine too many aspects of our domain logic into monolithic classes and methods. We will probably want to begin to tease out the different aspects of our domain logic into a Domain Model and wrap it with a series of Service Layers.

- The presentation layer is still relatively monolithic in nature. We may want to convert our view files to a Two Step View system. That will give us a unified layout across the entire application, provide a reusable series of "partial" templates, and help us reduce each view file to its central core.

- Our controllers may be handling several unrelated actions as an artifact of the legacy architecture. We may wish to reorganize them into more sensible groups for quicker understanding. Indeed, each controller may be doing too much work (i.e., a fat controller instead of a skinny one) that could better be handled by helper classes or a Service Layer.

- The response system combines the concerns of content building with HTTP response building. We may wish to refactor the entire response-sending process to two or more separate layers: one that deals with the body of the response and one that deals with the response headers. Indeed, we may wish to represent the response as a Data Transfer Object that describes our intentions, but leaves the actual response building-and-sending to a separate handler.

- The routing system is definitely transitional. We probably still depend on query parameters in the URL to pass client request information into the application, instead of using "pretty URLs" where the parameters are represented as parts of the path information. The routes themselves merely describe the class to be invoked, and do not carry as much information as they should about the action that the application should be executing. We will want to replace this basic router with a more powerful one.

- The front controller is acting as our dispatcher, instead of handing off route dispatch to a separate object. We may wish to separate the task of discovering the route information from the task of dispatching that route.

- Finally, our dependency injection container is very "manual" in nature. We may wish to find a container system that automates some of the more basic aspects of object creation, allowing us to concentrate on the more complex aspects of service definition.

In other words, we have the problems of a modern codebase, not a legacy one. We have traded the low-quality problems of a spaghetti mess for the "high-quality" problems of an autoloaded, dependency-injected, unit-tested, layer-separated, front-controlled codebase.

Because we have modernized our codebase, we can address these problems in a completely different way than we did under a legacy regime. We can bring the tools of Refactoring to bear against the code. Now that we have better separation of concerns, we can make small changes in limited sections of the code to improve the quality of that code. Each change can be tested for regressions via our unit test suite.

Each new feature that we add can be plugged into our new application architecture using the techniques we have acquired while modernizing it. No longer do we toss in a new page script copied-and-modified from some previous one. Instead, we add a unit-tested controller class and route to it through the front controller. New functionality in our domain logic is added as a unit-tested class or method in the domain layer. Changes and additions to presentation can be tested separately from our models and controllers via our view layer.

Conversion to Framework

There is also the possibility of converting our application over to the latest, hottest framework. Although switching to a public framework is a little bit like an application rewrite, it should be much easier now that we have a well-separated series of application layers. We should be able to determine which parts would be ported over to a public framework, and which are merely incidental to the operation of our particular architecture.

I advise neither for nor against this approach. I will only point out that, in the course of modernizing our legacy application, we have essentially built our own custom-tailored framework. We have done so with what is probably a more disciplined and rigorous approach than most public frameworks in PHP land. While we gain the community that goes along with a public framework, we also gain the baggage of the framework developers themselves. These and other tradeoffs are beyond my ability to judge on your behalf; you will have to decide for yourself if the benefits outweigh the costs.

Review and next steps

Regardless of how we proceed from here, there can be no doubt that the improvement of the *application* has led to an improvement in our quality of life and in our professional approach. The time we have invested in the code has paid off not only in terms of our employment, where we now spend less time feeling frustrated and demoralized, and more time feeling competent and productive. It has paid off in terms of our skills, our knowledge, and our experience regarding application architecture, patterns, and practices.

Our goals now are to continue improving our code, to continue improving ourselves, and to help others to improve as well. We need to share our knowledge. In doing so, we will reduce the amount of suffering in the world that comes from having to deal with legacy applications. As more people learn to apply what we have learned here, we can ourselves go on to bigger and better and more interesting issues in our professional lives.

So go forth and spread the good news to your colleagues, compatriots, and co-workers, that they need not suffer with legacy applications if they do not want to. They, can also modernize their codebases, and improve their own lives in doing so.

A
Typical Legacy Page Script

```php
<?php
2 include("common/db_include.php");
3 include("common/functions.inc");
4 include("theme/leftnav.php");
5 include("theme/header.php");
6
7 define("SEARCHNUM", 10);
8
9 function letter_links()
10 {
11 global $p, $letter;
12 $lettersArray = array(
13 '0-9', 'A', 'B', 'C', 'D', 'E', 'F', 'G', 'H', 'I',
14 'J', 'K', 'L', 'M', 'N', 'O', 'P', 'Q', 'R', 'S',
15 'T', 'U', 'V', 'W', 'X', 'Y', 'Z'
16 );
17 foreach ($lettersArray as $let) {
18 if ($letter == $let)
19 echo $let.' ';
20 else
21 echo '<a class="letters" '
22 . 'href="letter.php?p='
23 . $p
24 . '&letter='
25 . $let
26 . '">'
27 . $let
28 . '</a> ';
29 }
30 }
31
```

```
32 $page = ($page) ? $page : 0;
33
34 if (!empty($p) && $p!="all" && $p!="none") {
35 $where = "`foo` LIKE '%$p%'";
36 } else {
37 $where = "1";
38 }
39
40 if ($p=="hand") {
41 $where = "`foo` LIKE '%type1%'"
42 . " OR `foo` LIKE '%type2%'"
43 . " OR `foo` LIKE '%type3%'";
44 }
45
46 $where .= " AND `bar`='1'";
47 if ($s) {
48 $s = str_replace(" ", "%", $s);
49 $s = str_replace("'", "", $s);
50 $s = str_replace(";", "", $s);
51 $where .= " AND (`baz` LIKE '%$s%')";
52 $orderby = "ORDER BY `baz` ASC";
53 } elseif ($letter!="none" && $letter) {
54 $where .= " AND (`baz` LIKE '$letter%'"
55 . " OR `baz` LIKE 'The $letter%')";
56 $orderby = "ORDER BY `baz` ASC";
57 } else {
58 $orderby = "ORDER BY `item_date` DESC";
59 }
60 $query = mysql_query(
61 "SELECT * FROM `items` WHERE $where $orderby
62 LIMIT $page,".SEARCHNUM;
63 );
64 $count = db_count("items", $where);
65 ?>
66
67 <td align="middle" width="480" valign="top">
68 <img border="0" width="480" height="30"
69 src="http://example.com/images/example1.gif">
70 <table border="0" cellspacing="0" width="480"
71 cellpadding="0" bgcolor="#000000">
72 <tr>
73 <td colspan="2" width="480" height="50">
74 <img border="0"
```

```
75 src="http://example.com/images/example2.gif">
76 </td>
77 </tr>
78 <tr>
79 <td width="120" align="right" nowrap>
80 <img border="0"
81 src="http://example.com/images/example3.gif">
82 </td>
83 <td width="360" align="right" nowrap>
84 <div class="letter"><?php letter_links(); ?></div>
85 </td>
86 </tr>
87 </table>
88
89 <form name="search" enctype="multipart/form-data"
90 action="search.php" method="POST" margin="0"
91 style="margin: 0px;">
92 <table border="0" style="border-collapse: collapse"
93 width="480" cellpadding="0">
94 <tr>
95 <td align="center" width="140">
96 <input type="text" name="s" size="22"
97 class="user_search" title="enter your search..."
98 value="<?php
99 echo $s
100 ? $s
101 : "enter your search..."
102 ;
103 ?>" onFocus=" enable(this); "
104 onBlur=" disable(this); ">
105 </td>
106 <td align="center" width="70">
107 <input type="image" name="submit"
108 src="http://example.com/images/user_search.gif"
109 width="66" height="17">
110 </td>
111 <td align="right" width="135">
112 <img border="0"
113 src="http://example.com/images/list_foo.gif"
114 width="120" height="26">
115 </td>
116 <td align="center" width="135">
117 <select size="1" name="p" onChange="submit();">
118 <?php
```

```
119 if ($p) {
120 ${$p} = 'selected="selected"';
121 }
122 foreach ($foos as $key => $value) {
123 echo '<option value="'
124 . $key
125 . '" '
126 . ${$key}
127 . '>'
128 . $value
129 . '</option>';
130 }
131 ?>
132 </select>
133 </td>
134 </tr>
135 </table>
136 <?php if ($letter) {
137 echo '<input type="hidden" name="letter" '
138 . 'value="' . $letter . '">';
139 } ?>
140 </form>
141
142 <table border="0" cellspacing="0" width="480"
143 cellpadding="0" style="border-style: solid; border-color:
144 #606875; border-width: 1px 1px 0px 1px;">
145 <tr>
146 <td>
147 <div class="nav"><?php
148 $pagecount = ceil(($count / SEARCHNUM));
149 $currpage = ($page / SEARCHNUM) + 1;
150 if ($pagecount)
151 echo ($page + 1)
152 . " to "
153 . min(($page + SEARCHNUM), $count)
154 . " of $count";
155 ?></div>
156 </td>
157 <td align="right">
158 <div class="nav"><?php
159 unset($getstring);
160 if ($_POST) {
161 foreach ($_POST as $key => $val) {
162 if ($key != "page") {
```

```
163 $getstring .= "&$key=$val";
164 }
165 }
166 }
167 if ($_GET) {
168 foreach ($_GET as $key => $val) {
169 if ($key != "page") {
170 $getstring .= "&$key=$val";
171 }
172 }
173 }
174
175 if (!$pagecount) {
176 echo "No results found!";
177 } else {
178 if ($page >= (3*SEARCHNUM)) {
179 $firstlink = " | <a class=\"searchresults\"
180 href=\"?page=0$getstring\">1</a>";
181 if ($page >= (4*SEARCHNUM)) {
182 $firstlink .= " ... ";
183 }
184 }
185
186 if ($page >= (2*SEARCHNUM)) {
187 $prevpages = " | <a class=\"searchresults\""
188 . " href=\"?page="
189 . ($page - (2*SEARCHNUM))
190 . "$getstring\">"
191 . ($currpage - 2)
192 ."</a>";
193 }
194
195 if ($page >= SEARCHNUM) {
196 $prevpages .= " | <a class=\"searchresults\""
197 . " href=\"?page="
198 . ($page - SEARCHNUM)
199 . "$getstring\">"
200 . ($currpage - 1)
201 . "</a>";
202 }
203
204 if ($page==0) {
205 $prevlink = "&laquo; Previous";
206 } else {
```

```
207 $prevnum = $page - SEARCHNUM;
208 $prevlink = "<a class=\"searchresults\""
209 . " href=\"?page=$prevnum$getstring\">"
210 . "&laquo; Previous</a>";
211 }
212
213 if ($currpage==$pagecount) {
214 $nextlink = "Next &raquo;";
215 } else {
216 $nextnum = $page + SEARCHNUM;
217 $nextlink = "<a class=\"searchresults\""
218 . " href=\"?page=$nextnum$getstring\">"
219 . "Next &raquo;</a>";
220 }
221
222 if ($page < (($pagecount - 1) * SEARCHNUM))
223 $nextpages = " | <a class=\"searchresults\""
224 . " href=\"?page="
225 . ($page + SEARCHNUM)
226 . "$getstring\">"
227 . ($currpage + 1)
228 . "</a>";
229
230 if ($page < (($pagecount - 2)*SEARCHNUM)) {
231 $nextpages .= " | <a class=\"searchresults\""
232 . " href=\"?page="
233 . ($page + (2*SEARCHNUM))
234 . "$getstring\">"
235 . ($currpage + 2)
236 . "</a>";
237 }
238
239 if ($page < (($pagecount - 3)*SEARCHNUM)) {
240 if ($page < (($pagecount - 4)*SEARCHNUM))
241 $lastlink = " ... of ";
242 else
243 $lastlink = " | ";
244 $lastlink .= "<a class=\"searchresults\""
245 . href=\"?page="
246 . (($pagecount - 1)*SEARCHNUM)
247 . "$getstring\">"
248 . $pagecount
249 . "</a>";
250 }
```

```
251
252 $pagenums = " | <b>$currpage</b>";
253 echo $prevlink
254 . $firstlink
255 . $prevpages
256 . $pagenums
257 . $nextpages
258 . $lastlink
259 . ' | '
260 . $nextlink;
261 }
262 ?></div>
263 </td>
264 </tr>
265 </table>
266
267 <table border="0" cellspacing="0" width="100%"
268 cellpadding="0" style="border-style: solid; border-color:
269 #606875; border-width: 0px 1px 0px 1px;">
270
271 <?php while($item = mysql_fetch_array($query)) {
272
273 $links = get_links(
274 $item[id],
275 $item[filename],
276 $item[fileinfotext]
277 );
278
279 $dls = get_dls($item['id']);
280
281 echo '
282 <tr>
283 <td class="bg'.(($ii % 2) ? 1 : 2).'" align="center">
284
285 <div style="margin:10px">
286 <table border="0" style="border-collapse:
287 collapse" width="458" id="table5" cellpadding="0">
288 <tr>
289 <td rowspan="3" width="188">
290 <table border="0" cellpadding="0"
291 cellspacing="0" width="174">
292 <tr>
293 <td colspan="4">
294 <img border="0"
```

```
295 src="http://www.example.com/common/'
296 .$item[thumbnail].'"
297 width="178" height="74"
298 class="media_img">
299 </td>
300 </tr>
301 <tr>
302 <td style="border-color: #565656;
303 border-style: solid; border-width: 0px
304 0px 1px 1px;" width="18">
305 <a target="_blank"
306 href="'.$links[0][link].'"
307 '.$links[0][addlink].'>
308 <img border="0"
309 src="http://example.com/images/'
310 .$links[0][type].'.gif"
311 width="14" height="14"
312 hspace="3" vspace="3">
313 </a>
314 </td>
315 <td style="border-color: #565656;
316 border-style: solid; border-width: 0px
317 0px 1px 0px;" align="left" width="71">
318 <a target="_blank"
319 href="'.$links[0][link].'"
320 class="media_download_link"
321 '.$links[0][addlink].'>'
322 .(round($links[0][filesize]
323 / 104858) / 10).' MB</a>
324 </td>
325 <td style="border-color: #565656;
326 border-style: solid; border-width: 0px
327 0px 1px 0px;" width="18">
328 '.(($links[1][type]) ? '<a
329 target="_blank"
330 href="'.$links[1][link].'"
331 '.$links[1][addlink].'><img
332 border="0"
333 src="http://example.com/images/'
334 .$links[1][type].'.gif"
335 width="14" height="14" hspace="3"
336 vspace="3">
337 </td>
338 <td style="border-color: #565656;
```

```
r339 border-style: solid; border-width: 0px
340 1px 1px 0px;" align="left" width="71">
341 <a target="_blank"
342 href="'.$links[1][link].'"
343 class="media_download_link"
344 '.$links[1][addlink].'>'
345 .(round($links[1][filesize]
346 / 104858) / 10).' MB</a>' :
347 ' </td><td> ').'
348 </td>
349 </tr>
350 </table>
351 </td>
352 <td width="270" valign="bottom">
353 <div class="list_title">
354 <a
355 href="page.php?id='.$item[rel_id].'"
356 class="list_title_link">'.$item[baz].'</a>
357 </div>
358 </td>
359 </tr>
360 <tr>
361 <td align="left" width="270">
362 <div class="media_text">
363 '.$item[description].'
364 </div>
365 </td>
366 </tr>
367 <tr>
368 <td align="left" width="270">
369 <div class="media_downloads">'
370 .number_format($dls)
371 .' Downloads
372 </div>
373 </td>
374 </tr>
375 </table>
376 </div>
377 </td>
378 </tr>';
379 $ii++;
380 } ?>
381 </table>
382
```

```
383 <table border="0" cellspacing="0" width="480"
384 cellpadding="0" style="border-style: solid; border-color:
385 #606875; border-width: 0px 1px 1px 1px;">
386 <tr>
387 <td>
388 <div class="nav"><?php
389 if ($pagecount)
390 echo ($page + 1)
391 . " to "
392 . min(($page + SEARCHNUM), $count)
393 . " of $count";
394 ?></div>
395 </td>
396 <td align="right">
397 <div class="nav"><?php
398 if (!$pagecount) {
399 echo "No search results found!";
400 } else {
401 echo $prevlink
402 . $firstlink
403 . $prevpages
404 . $pagenums
405 . $nextpages
406 . $lastlink
407 . ' | '
408 . $nextlink;
409 }
410 ?></div>
411 </td>
412 </tr>
413 </table>
414 </td>
415
416 <?php include("theme/footer.php"); ?>
```

B

Code before Gateways

This appendix shows a partial page script for a legacy application. It has been sanitized and anonymized from an actual application.

This script was part of a system allowed journalism students to write articles for review, and to provide feedback on articles from fellow students. The students would offer "credits" for other students to review their work, and would receive credits from others by reviewing their articles. Because credits were paid per review, the students would limit the maximum number of reviews to make sure they did not run out of credits. Finally, they were allowed to provide notes indicating what the reviewer should pay attention to.

This is a version of the page script before being converted to using Gateway classes. It contains only the domain logic and data source interactions, not the preliminary setup or any display code.

```php
1 <?php
2 // ...
3 require 'includes/setup.php';
4 // ...
5
6 $article_types = array(1, 2, 3, 4, 5);
7 $failure = array();
8 $now = time();
9
10 // sanitize and escape the user input
11 $input = $_POST;
12 $input['body'] = strip_tags($input['body']);
13 $input['notes'] = strip_tags($input['notes']);
14 foreach ($input as $key => $val) {
15 $input[$key] = mysql_real_escape_string($val);
16 }
17
```

```
18 if (isset($input['ready']) && $input['ready'] == 'on') {
19 $input['ready'] = 1;
20 } else {
21 $input['ready'] = 0;
22 }
23
24 // nothing less than 0.01 credits per rating
25 $input['credits_per_rating'] = round(
26 $input['credits_per_rating'],
27 2
28 );
29
30 $credits = round(
31 $input['credits_per_rating'] * $input['max_ratings'],
32 2
33 );
34
35 // updating an existing article?
36 if ($input['id']) {
37
38 // make sure this article belongs to the user
39 $stm = "SELECT *
40 FROM articles
41 WHERE user_id = '{$user_id}'
42 AND id = '{$input['id']}'
43 LIMIT 1";
44 $result = mysql_query($stm);
45
46 if (mysql_num_rows($result)) {
47
48 // get the existing article from the database
49 $row = mysql_fetch_assoc($result);
50
51 // don't charge unless the article is ready
52 $decrement = false;
53
54 // is the article marked as ready?
55 if ($input['ready'] == 1) {
56
57 // did they offer at least the minimum?
58 if (
59 $credits > 0
60 && $input['credits_per_rating'] >= 0.01
61 && is_numeric($credits)
```

```
62 ) {
63
64 // was the article previously ready for review?
65 // (note 'row' not 'input')
66 if ($row['ready'] == 1) {
67
68 // only subtract (or add back) the difference to their
69 // account, since they already paid something
70 if (
71 is_numeric($row['credits_per_rating'])
72 && is_numeric($row['max_ratings'])
73 ) {
74 // user owes $credits, minus whatever they paid already
75 $amount = $row['credits_per_rating']
76 * $row['max_ratings']
77 $credits = $credits - $amount;
78 }
79
80 $decrement = true;
81
82 } else {
83 // article not ready previously, so they hadn't
84 // had credits deducted. if this is less than their
85 // in their account now, they may proceed.
86 $residual = $user->get('credits') - $credits;
87 $decrement = true;
88 }
89
90 } else {
91 $residual = -1;
92 $failure[] = "Credit offering invalid.";
93 $decrement = false;
94 }
95
96 } else {
97
98 // arbitrary positive value; they can proceed
99 $residual = 1;
100
101 // if it was previously ready but is no longer, refund them
102 if (
103 is_numeric($row['credits_per_rating'])
104 && is_numeric($row['max_ratings'])
105 && ($row['ready'] == 1)
```

```
106 ) {
107 // subtract a negative value
108 $amount = $row['credits_per_rating']
109 * $row['max_ratings']
110 $credits = -($amount);
111 $decrement = true;
112 }
113 }
114
115 if ($residual >= 0) {
116
117 if (strlen($input['notes'])>0) {
118 $notes = "notes = '{$input['notes']}'";
119 } else {
120 $notes = "notes = NULL";
121 }
122
123 if (strlen($input['title'])>0) {
124 $title = "title = '{$input['title']}'";
125 } else {
126 $title = "title = NULL";
127 }
128
129 if (! in_array(
130 $input['article_type'],
131 $article_types
132 )) {
133 $input['article_type'] = 1;
134 }
135
136 $stm = "UPDATE articles
137 SET
138 body = '{$input['body']}',
139 $notes,
140 $title,
141 article_type = '{$input['article_type']}',
142 ready = '{$input['ready']}',
143 last_edited = '{$now}',
144 ip = '{$_SERVER['REMOTE_ADDR']}',
145 credits_per_rating = '{$input['credits_per_rating']}',
146 max_ratings = '{$input['max_ratings']}'
147 WHERE user_id = '{$user_id}'
148 AND id = '{$input['id']}'";
149
```

```
150 if (mysql_query($stm)) {
151 $article_id = $input['id'];
152
153 if ($decrement) {
154 // Charge them
155 $stm = "UPDATE users
156 SET credits = credits - {$credits}
157 WHERE user_id = '{$user_id}'";
158 mysql_query($stm);
159 }
160 } else {
161 $failure[] = "Could not update article.";
162 }
163 } else {
164 $failure[] = "You do not have enough credits for ratings.";
165 }
166 }
167
168 } else {
169
170 // creating a new article. do not decrement until specified.
171 $decrement = false;
172
173 // if the article is ready, we need to subtract credits.
174 if ($input['ready'] == 1) {
175
176 // if this is greater than or equal to 0, they may proceed.
177 if (
178 $credits > 0
179 && $input['credits_per_rating']>=0.01
180 && is_numeric($credits)
181 ) {
182 // minimum offering is 0.01
183 $residual = $user->get('credits') - $credits;
184 $decrement = true;
185 } else {
186 $residual = -1;
187 $failure[] = "Credit offering invalid.";
188 }
189
190 } else {
191 // arbitrary positive value if they are not done with their
article.
192 // no deduction made yet.
```

```
193 $residual = 1;
194 }
195
196 // can user afford ratings on the new article?
197 if ($residual >= 0) {
198
199 // yes, insert the article
200 $stm = "INSERT INTO articles (
201 user_id,
202 ip,
203 last_edited,
204 article_type
205 ) VALUES (
206 '{$user_id}',
207 '{$_SERVER['REMOTE_ADDR']}',
208 '$now',
209 '$input['article_type']'
210 )";
211
212 if (mysql_query($stm)) {
213 $article_id = mysql_insert_id();
214 if ($decrement) {
215 // Charge them
216 $stm = "UPDATE users
217 SET credits = credits - {$credits}
218 WHERE user_id='{$user_id}'";
219 mysql_query($stm);
220 }
221 } else {
222 $failure[] = "Could not update credits.";
223 }
224
225 $stm = "UPDATE articles
226 SET
227 body = '{$input['body']}',
228 $notes,
229 $title,
230 article_type = '{$input['article_type']}',
231 ready = '{$input['ready']}',
232 last_edited = '$now',
233 ip = '{$_SERVER['REMOTE_ADDR']}',
234 credits_per_rating = '{$input['credits_per_rating']}',
235 max_ratings = '{$input['max_ratings']}'
236 WHERE
```

```
237 user_id = '{$user_id}'
238 AND id = '$article_id'
239 ";
240
241 if (! mysql_query($stm)) {
242 $failure[] = "Could not update article.";
243 }
244
245 } else {
246
247 // cannot afford ratings on new article
248 $failure[] = "You do not have enough credits for ratings.";
249 }
250 }
251 ?>
```

Code after Gateways

C

This appendix shows a version of the page script from Appendix B after being converted to use Gateway classes. Note how very little of it has changed. Even though the SQL statements have been removed, the domain business logic remains embedded in the page script.

The Gateway classes are provided below the page script, and show a conversion to PDO-style bound parameters. Also note that there have been minor modifications to the `if()` conditions in the page script: whereas previously they checked to see if a query succeeded, they now check for a return value from the Gateway.

page_script.php
```php
<?php
2 // ... $user_id value created earlier
3
4 $db = new Database($db_host, $db_user, $db_pass);
5 $articles_gateway = new ArticlesGateway($db);
6 $users_gateway = new UsersGateway($db);
7
8 $article_types = array(1, 2, 3, 4, 5);
9 $failure = array();
10 $now = time();
11
12 // sanitize and escape the user input
13 $input = $_POST;
14 $input['body'] = strip_tags($input['body']);
15 $input['notes'] = strip_tags($input['notes']);
16
17 if (isset($input['ready']) && $input['ready'] == 'on') {
18 $input['ready'] = 1;
19 } else {
20 $input['ready'] = 0;
21 }
```

```
22
23 // nothing less than 0.01 credits per rating
24 $input['credits_per_rating'] = round(
25 $input['credits_per_rating'],
26 2
27 );
28
29 $credits = round(
30 $input['credits_per_rating'] * $input['max_ratings'],
31 2
32 );
33
34 // updating an existing article?
35 if ($input['id']) {
36
37 $row = $articles_gateway->selectOneByIdAndUserId($input['id'],
$user_id);
38
39 if ($row) {
40
41 // don't charge unless the article is ready
42 $decrement = false;
43
44 // is the article marked as ready?
45 if ($input['ready'] == 1) {
46
47 // did they offer at least the minimum?
48 if (
49 $credits > 0
50 && $input['credits_per_rating'] >= 0.01
51 && is_numeric($credits)
52 ) {
53
54 // was the article previously ready for review?
55 // (note 'row' not 'input')
56 if ($row['ready'] == 1) {
57
58 // only subtract (or add back) the difference to their
59 // account, since they already paid something
60 if (
61 is_numeric($row['credits_per_rating'])
62 && is_numeric($row['max_ratings'])
63 ) {
```

```
64 // user owes $credits, minus whatever they paid already
65 $amount = $row['credits_per_rating']
66 * $row['max_ratings']
67 $credits = $credits - $amount;
68 }
69
70 $decrement = true;
71
72 } else {
73 // article not ready previously, so they hadn't
74 // had credits deducted. if this is less than their
75 // in their account now, they may proceed.
76 $residual = $user->get('credits') - $credits;
77 $decrement = true;
78 }
79
80 } else {
81 $residual = -1;
82 $failure[] = "Credit offering invalid.";
83 $decrement = false;
84 }
85
86 } else {
87
88 // arbitrary positive value; they can proceed
89 $residual = 1;
90
91 // if it was previously ready but is no longer, refund them
92 if (
93 is_numeric($row['credits_per_rating'])
94 && is_numeric($row['max_ratings'])
95 && ($row['ready'] == 1)
96 ) {
97 // subtract a negative value
98 $amount = $row['credits_per_rating']
99 * $row['max_ratings']
100 $credits = -($amount);
101 $decrement = true;
102 }
103 }
104
105 if ($residual >= 0) {
106
```

```
107 $input['ip'] = $_SERVER['REMOTE_ADDR'];
108 $input['last_edited'] = $now;
109
110 if (! in_array(
111 $input['article_type'],
112 $article_types
113 )) {
114 $input['article_type'] = 1;
115 }
116
117 $result = $articles_gateway->updateByIdAndUserId(
118 $input['id'],
119 $user_id,
120 $input
121 );
122
123 if ($result) {
124 $article_id = $input['id'];
125
126 if ($decrement) {
127 $users_gateway->decrementCredits($user_id, $credits);
128 }
129 } else {
130 $failure[] = "Could not update article.";
131 }
132 } else {
133 $failure[] = "You do not have enough credits for ratings.";
134 }
135 }
136
137 } else {
138
139 // creating a new article. do not decrement until specified.
140 $decrement = false;
141
142 // if the article is ready, we need to subtract credits.
143 if ($input['ready'] == 1) {
144
145 // if this is greater than or equal to 0, they may proceed.
146 if (
147 $credits > 0
148 && $input['credits_per_rating']>=0.01
149 && is_numeric($credits)
150 ) {
```

```
151 // minimum offering is 0.01
152 $residual = $user->get('credits') - $credits;
153 $decrement = true;
154 } else {
155 $residual = -1;
156 $failure[] = "Credit offering invalid.";
157 }
158
159 } else {
160 // arbitrary positive value if they are not done with their
article.
161 // no deduction made yet.
162 $residual = 1;
163 }
164
165 // can user afford ratings on the new article?
166 if ($residual >= 0) {
167
168 // yes, insert the article
169 $input['last_edited'] = $now;
170 $input['ip'] = $_SERVER['REMOTE_ADDR'];
171 $article_id = $articles_gateway->insert($input);
172
173 if ($article_id) {
174 if ($decrement) {
175 // Charge them
176 $users_gateway->decrementCredits($user_id, $credits);
177 }
178 } else {
179 $failure[] = "Could not update credits.";
180 }
181
182 $result = $articles_gateway->updateByIdAndUserId(
183 $article_id,
184 $user_id,
185 $input
186 );
187
188 if (! $result) {
189 $failure[] = "Could not update article.";
190 }
191
192 } else {
193
```

```
194 // cannot afford ratings on new article
195 $failure[] = "You do not have enough credits for ratings.";
196 }
197 }
198 ?>
```

classes/Domain/Articles/ArticlesGateway.php

```
1 <?php
2 namespace Domain\Articles;
3
4 class ArticlesGateway
5 {
6 protected $db;
7
8 public function __construct(Database $db)
9 {
10 $this->db = $db;
11 }
12
13 public function selectOneByIdAndUserId($id, $user_id)
14 {
15 $stm = "SELECT *
16 FROM articles
17 WHERE user_id = :user_id
18 AND id = :id
19 LIMIT 1";
20
21 return $this->db->query($stm, array(
22 'id' => $id,
23 'user_id' => $user_id,
24 ))
25 }
26
27 public function updateByIdAndUserId($id, $user_id, $input)
28 {
29 if (strlen($input['notes']) > 0) {
30 $notes = "notes = :notes";
31 } else {
32 $notes = "notes = NULL";
33 }
34
35 if (strlen($input['title']) > 0) {
```

```
36 $title = "title = :title";
37 } else {
38 $title = "title = NULL";
39 }
40
41 $input['id'] = $id;
42 $input['user_id'] = $user_id;
43
44 $stm = "UPDATE articles
45 SET
46 body = :body,
47 $notes,
48 $title,
49 article_type = :article_type,
50 ready = :ready,
51 last_edited = :last_edited,
52 ip = :ip,
53 credits_per_rating = :credits_per_rating,
54 max_ratings = :max_ratings
55 WHERE user_id = :user_id
56 AND id = :id";
57
58 return $this->query($stm, $input);
59 }
60
61 public function insert($input)
62 {
63 $stm = "INSERT INTO articles (
64 user_id,
65 ip,
66 last_edited,
67 article_type
68 ) VALUES (
69 :user_id,
70 :ip,
71 :last_edited,
72 :article_type
73 )";
74 $this->db->query($stm, $input);
75 return $this->db->lastInsertId();
76 }
77 }
78 ?>
```

classes/Domain/Users/UsersGateway.php

```php
1 <?php
2 namespace Domain\Users;
3
4 class UsersGateway
5 {
6 protected $db;
7
8 public function __construct(Database $db)
9 {
10 $this->db = $db;
11 }
12
13 public function decrementCredits($user_id, $credits)
14 {
15 $stm = "UPDATE users
16 SET credits = credits - :credits
17 WHERE user_id = :user_id";
18 $this->db->query($stm, array(
19 'user_id' => $user_id,
20 'credits' => $credits,
21 ));
22 }
23 }
24 ?>
```

D
Code after Transaction Scripts

This Appendix shows a version of the code from appendices B and C that extracts the domain logic from the page script into a *Transactions* class. Note how the original page script is now reduced to being a object creation and injection mechanism, and hands off most logic to the *Transactions* classes. Note also how the `$failure`, `$credits`, and `$article_types` variables are now properties on the Transactions class, and how the normalization/sanitizing logic and credit-calculation logic is part of the *Transactions* logic.

page_script.php
```php
<?php
2
3 // ... $user_id value created earlier
4
5 $db = new Database($db_host, $db_user, $db_pass);
6 $articles_gateway = new ArticlesGateway($db);
7 $users_gateway = new UsersGateway($db);
8 $article_transactions = new ArticleTransactions(
9 $articles_gateway,
10 $users_gateway
11 );
12
13 if ($_POST['id']) {
14 $article_transactions->updateExistingArticle($user_id, $_POST);
15 } else {
16 $article_transactions->submitNewArticle($user_id, $_POST);
17 }
18
```

```
19 $failure = $article_transactions->getFailure();
20 ?>
```

classes/Domain/Articles/ArticleTransactions.php

```php
1 <?php
2 namespace Domain\Articles;
3
4 use Domain\Users\UsersGateway;
5
6 class ArticleTransactions
7 {
8 protected $article_types = array(1, 2, 3, 4, 5);
9
10 protected $failure = array();
11
12 protected $input = array();
13
14 public function __construct(
15 ArticlesGateway $articles_gateway,
16 UsersGateway $users_gateway
17 ) {
18 $this->articles_gateway = $articles_gateway;
19 $this->users_gateway = $users_gateway;
20 }
21
22 public function getInput()
23 {
24 return $this->input;
25 }
26
27 public function getFailure()
28 {
29 return $this->failure;
30 }
31
32 public function getCredits()
33 {
34 return round(
35 $this->input['credits_per_rating'] * $this->input['max_ratings'],
36 2
37 );
38 }
39
40 public function filterInput($input)
```

```
41 {
42 $input['body'] = strip_tags($input['body']);
43 $input['notes'] = strip_tags($input['notes']);
44
45 if (isset($input['ready']) && $input['ready'] == 'on') {
46 $input['ready'] = 1;
47 } else {
48 $input['ready'] = 0;
49 }
50
51 // nothing less than 0.01 credits per rating
52 $input['credits_per_rating'] = round(
53 $input['credits_per_rating'],
54 2
55 );
56
57 // return the filtered input
58 return $input;
59 }
60
61 public function updateExistingArticle($user_id, $input)
62 {
63 $this->input = $this->filterInput($input);
64 $now = time();
65 $this->failure = array();
66 $credits = $this->getCredits();
67
68 $row = $this->articles_gateway->selectOneByIdAndUserId(
69 $this->input['id'],
70 $user_id
71 );
72
73 if ($row) {
74
75 // don't charge unless the article is ready
76 $decrement = false;
77
78 // is the article marked as ready?
79 if ($this->input['ready'] == 1) {
80
81 // did they offer at least the minimum?
82 if (
83 $credits > 0
84 && $this->input['credits_per_rating'] >= 0.01
```

```
 85 && is_numeric($credits)
 86 ) {
 87
 88 // was the article previously ready for review?
 89 // (note 'row' not 'input')
 90 if ($row['ready'] == 1) {
 91
 92 // only subtract (or add back) the difference to their
 93 // account, since they already paid something
 94 if (
 95 is_numeric($row['credits_per_rating'])
 96 && is_numeric($row['max_ratings'])
 97 ) {
 98 // user owes $credits, minus whatever they paid
 99 // already
100 $amount = $row['credits_per_rating']
101 * $row['max_ratings']
102 $credits = $credits - $amount;
103 }
104
105 $decrement = true;
106
107 } else {
108 // article not ready previously, so they hadn't
109 // had credits deducted. if this is less than their
110 // in their account now, they may proceed.
111 $residual = $user->get('credits') - $credits;
112 $decrement = true;
113 }
114
115 } else {
116 $residual = -1;
117 $this->failure[] = "Credit offering invalid.";
118 $decrement = false;
119 }
120
121 } else {
122
123 // arbitrary positive value; they can proceed
124 $residual = 1;
125
126 // if it was previously ready but is no longer, refund them
127 if (
128 is_numeric($row['credits_per_rating'])
```

```
129 && is_numeric($row['max_ratings'])
130 && ($row['ready'] == 1)
131 ) {
132 // subtract a negative value
133 $amount = $row['credits_per_rating']
134 * $row['max_ratings']
135 $credits = -($amount);
136 $decrement = true;
137 }
138 }
139
140 if ($residual >= 0) {
141
142 $this->input['ip'] = $_SERVER['REMOTE_ADDR'];
143 $this->input['last_edited'] = $now;
144
145 if (! in_array(
146 $this->input['article_type'],
147 $this->article_types
148 )) {
149 $this->input['article_type'] = 1;
150 }
151
152 $result = $this->articles_gateway->updateByIdAndUserId(
153 $this->input['id'],
154 $user_id,
155 $this->input
156 );
157
158 if ($result) {
159 $article_id = $this->input['id'];
160
161 if ($decrement) {
162 $this->users_gateway->decrementCredits(
163 $user_id,
164 $credits
165 );
166 }
167 } else {
168 $this->failure[] = "Could not update article.";
169 }
170 } else {
171 $this->failure[] = "You do not have enough credits for ratings.";
172 }
```

```
173 }
174 }
175
176 public function submitNewArticle($user_id, $input)
177 {
178 $this->input = $this->filterInput($input);
179 $now = time();
180 $this->failure = array();
181 $credits = $this->getCredits();
182
183 $decrement = false;
184
185 // if the article is ready, we need to subtract credits.
186 if ($this->input['ready'] == 1) {
187
188 // if this is greater than or equal to 0, they may proceed.
189 if (
190 $credits > 0
191 && $this->input['credits_per_rating']>=0.01
192 && is_numeric($credits)
193 ) {
194 // minimum offering is 0.01
195 $residual = $user->get('credits') - $credits;
196 $decrement = true;
197 } else {
198 $residual = -1;
199 $this->failure[] = "Credit offering invalid.";
200 }
201
202 } else {
203 // arbitrary positive value if they are not done with their
article.
204 // no deduction made yet.
205 $residual = 1;
206 }
207
208 // can user afford ratings on the new article?
209 if ($residual >= 0) {
210
211 // yes, insert the article
212 $this->input['last_edited'] = $now;
213 $this->input['ip'] = $_SERVER['REMOTE_ADDR'];
214 $article_id = $this->articles_gateway->insert($this->input);
215
```

```
216 if ($article_id) {
217 if ($decrement) {
218 // Charge them
219 $this->users_gateway->decrementCredits($user_id, $credits);
220 }
221 } else {
222 $this->failure[] = "Could not update credits.";
223 }
224
225 $result = $this->articles_gateway->updateByIdAndUserId(
226 $article_id,
227 $user_id,
228 $this->input
229 );
230
231 if (! $result) {
232 $this->failure[] = "Could not update article.";
233 }
234
235 } else {
236
237 // cannot afford ratings on new article
238 $this->failure[] = "You do not have enough credits for ratings.";
239 }
240 }
241 }
242 ?>
```

E
Code before Collecting
Presentation Logic

articles.php

```php
1 <?php
2 require "includes/setup.php";
3
4 $current_page = 'articles';
5
6 include "header.php";
7
8 $id = isset($_GET['id']) ? $_GET['id'] : 0;
9 if ($id) {
10 $page_title = "Edit An Article";
11 } else {
12 $page_title = "Submit An Article";
13 }
14
15 ?><h1><?php echo $page_title ?></h1><?php
16
17 $user_id = $user->getId();
18
19 $db = new Database($db_host, $db_user, $db_pass);
20 $articles_gateway = new ArticlesGateway($db);
21 $users_gateway = new UsersGateway($db);
22 $article_transactions = new ArticleTransactions(
23 $articles_gateway,
24 $users_gateway
25 );
26
27 if ($id) {
```

```
28 $article_transactions->updateExistingArticle($user_id, $_POST);
29 } else {
30 $article_transactions->submitNewArticle($user_id, $_POST);
31 }
32
33 $failure = $article_transactions->getFailure();
34 $input = $article_transactions->getInput();
35
36 ?>
37
38 <?php
39 if ($failure) {
40 $failure_text = implode("<br />\n", $failure);
41 echo "<h2>Failure</h2>";
42 echo "<p>We could not save the article.<br />";
43 echo $failure_text. "</p>";
44 } else {
45 echo "
46 <h2>Success</h2>
47 <p>We saved the article.</p>
48 ";
49 }
50 ?>
51
52 <form method="POST" action="<?php echo $_SERVER['PHP_SELF']?>">
53
54 <input type="hidden" name="id" value="<?php echo $id ?>" />
55
56 <h3>Title</h3>
57 <input type="text" name="title" value="<?php
58 echo $input['title']
59 ?>" size="100">
60
61
62 <h3>Article</h3>
63 <textarea name="body" cols="80" rows="30"><?php
64 echo stripslashes($input['body'])
65 ?></textarea>
66
67 <h3>Ratings</h3>
68 <p>How many rated reviews do you want?</p>
69 <select name='max_ratings'>
70 <?php for ($i = 1; $i <= 10; $i ++) {
71 echo "<option value='$i' ";
```

```
72 if ($input['max_ratings'] == $i) {
73 echo 'selected="selected"';
74 }
75 echo ">$i</option>\n";
76 } ?>
77 </select>
78
79 <p>How many credits will you give for each rating?</p>
80 <input type='text' name='credits_per_rating' value='<?php
81 echo $input['credits_per_rating'];
82 ?>' size='5' />
83
84 <h3>Notes for Reviewers</h3>
85 <input type="text" name="notes" value="<?php
86 echo $input['notes']
87 ?>" size="100">
88 <label><input type="checkbox" name="ready" <?php
89 echo $input['ready'] ? 'checked="checked"' : '';
90 ?> /> This article is ready to be rated.</label>
91
92 <p align="center">
93 <input type="submit" value="Save" name="submit">
94 </p>
95
96 </form>
97
98 <?php
99 include "footer.php";
100 ?>
```

F
Code after Collecting Presentation Logic

articles.php

```php
1 <?php
2 require "includes/setup.php";
3
4 $user_id = $user->getId();
5
6 $db = new Database($db_host, $db_user, $db_pass);
7 $articles_gateway = new ArticlesGateway($db);
8 $users_gateway = new UsersGateway($db);
9 $article_transactions = new ArticleTransactions(
10 $articles_gateway,
11 $users_gateway
12 );
13
14 $id = isset($_GET['id']) ? $_GET['id'] : 0;
15 if ($id) {
16 $article_transactions->updateExistingArticle($user_id, $_POST);
17 } else {
18 $article_transactions->submitNewArticle($user_id, $_POST);
19 }
20
21 $failure = $article_transactions->getFailure();
22 $input = $article_transactions->getInput();
23 $action = $_SERVER['PHP_SELF'];
24
25 /** PRESENTATION */
26
27 $current_page = 'articles';
```

```php
28
29 include "header.php";
30
31 if ($id) {
32 $page_title = "Edit An Article";
33 } else {
34 $page_title = "Submit An Article";
35 }
36 ?>
37
38 <h1><?php echo $page_title ?></h1><?php
39
40 if ($failure) {
41 $failure_text = implode("<br />\n", $failure);
42 echo "<h2>Failure</h2>";
43 echo "<p>We could not save the article.<br />";
44 echo $failure_text. "</p>";
45 } else {
46 echo "
47 <h2>Success</h2>
48 <p>We saved the article.</p>
49 ";
50 }
51 ?>
52
53 <form method="POST" action="<?php echo $action ?>">
54
55 <input type="hidden" name="id" value="<?php echo $id ?>" />
56
57 <h3>Title</h3>
58 <input type="text" name="title" value="<?php
59 echo $input['title']
60 ?>" size="100">
61
62
63 <h3>Article</h3>
64 <textarea name="body" cols="80" rows="30"><?php
65 echo stripslashes($input['body'])
66 ?></textarea>
67
68 <h3>Ratings</h3>
69 <p>How many rated reviews do you want?</p>
70 <select name='max_ratings'>
71 <?php for ($i = 1; $i <= 10; $i ++) {
```

```
72 echo "<option value='$i' ";
73 if ($input['max_ratings'] == $i) {
74 echo 'selected="selected"';
75 }
76 echo ">$i</option>\n";
77 } ?>
78 </select>
79
80 <p>How many credits will you give for each rating?</p>
81 <input type='text' name='credits_per_rating' value='<?php
82 echo $input['credits_per_rating'];
83 ?>' size='5' />
84
85 <h3>Notes for Reviewers</h3>
86 <input type="text" name="notes" value="<?php
87 echo $input['notes']
88 ?>" size="100">
89 <label><input type="checkbox" name="ready" <?php
90 echo $input['ready'] ? 'checked="checked"' : '';
91 ?> /> This article is ready to be rated.</label>
92
93 <p align="center">
94 <input type="submit" value="Save" name="submit">
95 </p>
96
97 </form>
98
99 <?php
100 include "footer.php";
101 ?>
```

G
Code after Response
View File

articles.php

```php
1 <?php
2 require "includes/setup.php";
3
4 $user_id = $user->getId();
5
6 $db = new Database($db_host, $db_user, $db_pass);
7 $articles_gateway = new ArticlesGateway($db);
8 $users_gateway = new UsersGateway($db);
9 $article_transactions = new ArticleTransactions(
10 $articles_gateway,
11 $users_gateway
12 );
13
14 $id = isset($_GET['id']) ? $_GET['id'] : 0;
15 if ($id) {
16 $article_transactions->updateExistingArticle($user_id, $_POST);
17 } else {
18 $article_transactions->submitNewArticle($user_id, $_POST);
19 }
20
21 $response = new \Mlaphp\Response('/path/to/app/views');
22 $response->setView('articles.html.php');
23 $response->setVars(array(
24 'id' => $id,
25 'failure' => $article_transactions->getFailure(),
26 'input' => $article_transactions->getInput(),
27 'action' => $_SERVER['PHP_SELF'],
```

```
28 ));
29 $response->send();
30 ?>
```

views/articles.html.php

```
1 <?php
2 $current_page = 'articles';
3
4 include "header.php";
5
6 if ($id) {
7 $page_title = "Edit An Article";
8 } else {
9 $page_title = "Submit An Article";
10 }
11 ?>
12
13 <h1><?php echo $page_title ?></h1><?php
14
15 if ($failure) {
16 echo "<h2>Failure</h2>";
17 echo "<p>We could not save the article.<br />";
18 foreach ($failure as $failure_text) {
19 echo $this->esc($failure_text) . "<br />";
20 }
21 echo "</p>";
22 } else {
23 echo "
24 <h2>Success</h2>
25 <p>We saved the article.</p>
26 ";
27 }
28 ?>
29
30 <form method="POST" action="<?php echo $this->esc($action) ?>">
31
32 <input type="hidden" name="id" value="<?php echo $this->esc($id)
?>" />
33
34 <h3>Title</h3>
35 <input type="text" name="title" value="<?php
36 echo $this->esc($input['title'])
37 ?>" size="100">
38
39
```

```
40 <h3>Article</h3>
41 <textarea name="body" cols="80" rows="30"><?php
42 echo stripslashes($this->esc($input['body']))
43 ?></textarea>
44
45 <h3>Ratings</h3>
46 <p>How many rated reviews do you want?</p>
47 <select name='max_ratings'>
48 <?php for ($i = 1; $i <= 10; $i ++) {
49 $i = $this->esc($i);
50 echo "<option value='$i' ";
51 if ($input['max_ratings'] == $i) {
52 echo 'selected="selected"';
53 }
54 echo ">$i</option>\n";
55 } ?>
56 </select>
57
58 <p>How many credits will you give for each rating?</p>
59 <input type='text' name='credits_per_rating' value='<?php
60 echo $this->esc($input['credits_per_rating']);
61 ?>' size='5' />
62
63 <h3>Notes for Reviewers</h3>
64 <input type="text" name="notes" value="<?php
65 echo $this->esc($input['notes'])
66 ?>" size="100">
67 <label><input type="checkbox" name="ready" <?php
68 echo ($input['ready']) ? 'checked="checked"' : '';
69 ?> /> This article is ready to be rated.</label>
70
71 <p align="center">
72 <input type="submit" value="Save" name="submit">
73 </p>
74
75 </form>
76
77 <?php
78 include "footer.php";
79 ?>
```

H
Code after Controller Rearrangement

articles.php

```php
1 <?php
2 require "includes/setup.php";
3
4 /* DEPENDENCY */
5
6 $db = new Database($db_host, $db_user, $db_pass);
7 $articles_gateway = new ArticlesGateway($db);
8 $users_gateway = new UsersGateway($db);
9 $article_transactions = new ArticleTransactions(
10 $articles_gateway,
11 $users_gateway
12 );
13 $response = new \Mlaphp\Response('/path/to/app/views');
14
15 /* CONTROLLER */
16
17 $user_id = $user->getId();
18
19 $id = isset($_GET['id']) ? $_GET['id'] : 0;
20 if ($id) {
21 $article_transactions->updateExistingArticle($user_id, $_POST);
22 } else {
23 $article_transactions->submitNewArticle($user_id, $_POST);
24 }
25
26 $response->setView('articles.html.php');
```

```
27 $response->setVars(array(
28 'id' => $id,
29 'failure' => $article_transactions->getFailure(),
30 'input' => $article_transactions->getInput(),
31 'action' => $_SERVER['PHP_SELF'],
32 ));
33
34 /* FINISHED */
35
36 $response->send();
37 ?>
```

I
Code after Controller Extraction

articles.php

```php
1 <?php
2 require "includes/setup.php";
3
4 /* DEPENDENCY */
5
6 $db = new Database($db_host, $db_user, $db_pass);
7 $articles_gateway = new ArticlesGateway($db);
8 $users_gateway = new UsersGateway($db);
9 $article_transactions = new ArticleTransactions(
10 $articles_gateway,
11 $users_gateway
12 );
13 $response = new \Mlaphp\Response('/path/to/app/views');
14 $controller = new \Controller\ArticlesPage();
15
16 /* CONTROLLER */
17
18 $response = $controller->__invoke(
19 $request,
20 $response,
21 $user,
22 $article_transactions
23 );
24
25 /* FINISHED */
26
27 $response->send();
```

```
28 ?>
```

classes/Controller/ArticlesPage.php

```php
1 <?php
2 namespace Controller;
3
4 use Domain\Articles\ArticleTransactions;
5 use Mlaphp\Request;
6 use Mlaphp\Response;
7 use User;
8
9 class ArticlesPage
10 {
11 public function __construct()
12 {
13 }
14
15 public function __invoke(
16 Request $request,
17 Response $response,
18 User $user,
19 ArticleTransactions $article_transactions
20 ) {
21 $user_id = $user->getId();
22
23 $id = isset($request->get['id'])
24 ? $request->get['id']
25 : 0;
26
27 if ($id) {
28 $article_transactions->updateExistingArticle(
29 $user_id,
30 $request->post
31 );
32 } else {
33 $article_transactions->submitNewArticle(
34 $user_id,
35 $request->post
36 );
37 }
38
39 $response->setView('articles.html.php');
40 $response->setVars(array(
41 'id' => $id,
```

```
42 'failure' => $article_transactions->getFailure(),
43 'input' => $article_transactions->getInput(),
44 'action' => $request->server['PHP_SELF'],
45 ));
46
47 return $response;
48 }
49 }
50 ?>
```

J
Code after Controller Dependency Injection

articles.php

```php
1 <?php
2 require "includes/setup.php";
3
4 /* DEPENDENCY */
5
6 $db = new Database($db_host, $db_user, $db_pass);
7 $articles_gateway = new ArticlesGateway($db);
8 $users_gateway = new UsersGateway($db);
9 $article_transactions = new ArticleTransactions(
10 $articles_gateway,
11 $users_gateway
12 );
13 $response = new \Mlaphp\Response('/path/to/app/views');
14 $controller = new \Controller\ArticlesPage(
15 $request,
16 $response,
17 $user,
18 $article_transactions
19 );
20
21 /* CONTROLLER */
22
23 $response = $controller->__invoke();
24
25 /* FINISHED */
26
27 $response->send();
28 ?>
```

classes/Controller/ArticlesPage.php

```php
1 <?php
2 namespace Controller;
3
4 use Domain\Articles\ArticleTransactions;
5 use Mlaphp\Request;
6 use Mlaphp\Response;
7 use User;
8
9 class ArticlesPage
10 {
11 protected $user;
12
13 protected $article_transactions;
14
15 protected $request;
16
17 protected $response;
18
19 public function __construct(
20 Request $request,
21 Response $response,
22 User $user,
23 ArticleTransactions $article_transactions
24 ) {
25 $this->user = $user;
26 $this->article_transactions = $article_transactions;
27 $this->request = $request;
28 $this->response = $response;
29 }
30
31 public function __invoke()
32 {
33 $user_id = $this->user->getId();
34
35 $id = isset($this->request->get['id'])
36 ? $this->request->get['id']
37 : 0;
38
39 if ($id) {
40 $article_transactions->updateExistingArticle(
41 $user_id,
42 $this->request->post
43 );
```

```
44 } else {
```
```
45 $article_transactions->submitNewArticle(
46 $user_id,
47 $this->request->post
48 );
49 }
50
51 $this->response->setView('articles.html.php');
52 $this->response->setVars(array(
53 'id' => $id,
54 'failure' => $this->article_transactions->getFailure(),
55 'input' => $this->article_transactions->getInput(),
56 'action' => $this->request->server['PHP_SELF'],
57 ));
58
59 return $this->response;
60 }
61 }
62 ?>
```

Index

Symbols

A

B

C

cross-site scripting (XSS)
  about 126
  reference 127
custom autoloader
  using 21

D

Database class 105-107
definition file
  logic, executing 36
  similar class names 38
DELETE statement 93, 94
dependency injection
  about 43
  automating 70
  extra code 68
  issues 58
  replacement process 59
dependency injection container
  about 185, 186
  adding 186, 187
  front controller, modifying 189, 190
  include file, adding 187
  page scripts, extracting to services 190
  reference link 185
  router service, adding 188
domain 109
domain logic
  echo 118
  in Gateway classes 119
  in non-domain classes 119
  print 118
domain logic patterns
  about 110-112
  checking 117
  code, checking 116
  committing 117
  domain model 110
  extracted transactions, testing 116
  extracting 112, 113
  extraction, example 114-116
  Gateway calls, testing 117
  Gateway classes, searching 113
  relevant domain logic, discovering 113, 114
  relevant domain logic, extracting 113, 114
  service layer 111

table module 110
transaction script 110

E

editor/IDE 12
embedded action logic
  about 143
  action logic, moving 147
  class name, picking 146
  code blocks, identifying 145
  code, committing 149
  code, moving to related block 145
  Controller class, extracting 146
  Controller, converting to dependency
      injection 148
  Controller test, writing 149
  extraction process 144
  extraction process, performing 149
  include calls, in controller block 151
  multiple actions, performing with
      Controller 151
  page script, rearranging 144
  parameters, passing to Controller
      method 149, 150
  QA, notifying 149
  rearranged code, spot checking 145
  searching 144
  Skeleton class file, creating 146
  spot check, rearranging 144
  tests, pushing to repository 149
embedded domain logic 110
embedded include calls 153, 154
embedded instantiation 57, 58
embedded presentation logic
  about 121, 122
  business logic 140
  class methods 139
  content, streaming 135-137
  extraction process 122, 123
  page script, rearranging 123, 124
  presentation variables 137, 138
  reviewing 141
  searching for 123
  spot check, rearranging 123, 124
  template system 134, 135
  view files tests, writing 128

embedded SQL statements
about 83, 84
extraction process 84
Gateway class method 87, 88
SQL statements, searching 85
exceptions 64

F

factory
collections, creating 69
Factory object 58
file structure 2, 3
framework
legacy application, converting 201
front controller
modifying 189, 190
function
inline definition 36
function file conversion, to class file
about 31, 32
class file, moving 33
function calls, changing to static
method calls 33
static method calls, spot checking 33
functions, consolidating into class files
about 30
candidate include, searching 31
function file, converting to class file 31, 32
single class file, converting from include
to autoloading 34

G

Gateway class
code 221
domain logic 119
SQL statements, extracting 85
Gateway class method
about 87, 88
code, replacing 92
committing 92
pushing 92
SQL Injection, defeating 88-90
SQL statements, searching 93
testing 92
test, writing 90, 91

global dependencies
checking 50
classes, converting to use dependency
injection 50
creating 43-45
global properties, converting to
constructor parameters 47
global variable, converting to properties 46
global variable, searching 46
QA, notifying 50
replacement process 45
testing 47
global properties
converting, to constructor parameters 47
instantiations, converting 48, 49
global variable
converting, to properties 46
searching 46

H

headers 132

I

include calls
code, refactoring 160
committing 162
coupled variables, discovering through
testing 158, 159
Dependency Injection, converting 160-162
include calls, replacing 163
include calls, searching 156
include file, copying to class method 157
include file, deleting 160
multiple class, defining 35
multiple include calls, replacing 157
original include call, replacing 157
originating, in non-class files 163
other include calls, replacing 160
pushing 162
replacement process 155
single include call, replacing 156
test, deleting 160
test, replacing 160
test, writing 160
include files
logic, receiving in class 163

transactions
  approaches 118, 119
Transactions class
  code logic 229

U

UPDATE statement 93, 94
URL paths, decoupling process
  about 172
  committing 177
  coordinating 177
  front controller, creating 172, 173
  operations, coordinating with 172
  page scripts, moving 176, 177
  pages/ directory, creating 173
  pushing 177
  server, reconfiguring 175, 176
  spot checking 176

V

variables
  retaining 188
  with class names 52, 53
view file tests
  code, committing 132
  code, pushing to repository 132
  correctness of content, asserting 130-132
  presentation logic, searching 132
  QA, notifying 132
  tests/views/ directory 128
  writing 128-130

Z

Zend\Escaper
  URL 128

www.ingramcontent.com/pod-product-compliance
Lightning Source LLC
Chambersburg PA
CBHW080520220326
41599CB00032B/6145